YOU & YOUR TODDLER

3

Dr. Miriam Stoppard

YOU & YOUR TODDLER

HEALTHCARE

DORLING KINDERSLEY

LONDON, NEW YORK, MUNICH,
MELBOURNE AND DELHI

DESIGN & EDITORIAL   Mason Linklater

SENIOR MANAGING ART EDITOR   Lynne Brown
SENIOR MANAGING EDITOR   Corinne Roberts

SENIOR ART EDITOR   Karen Ward
SENIOR EDITOR   Penny Warren

PRODUCTION   Sarah Coltman

First published in Great Britain in 1999 by
Dorling Kindersley Limited, 80 Strand,
London WC2R 0RL
A Penguin Company

Reprinted 2001

Some material in this book was previously published by Dorling
Kindersley in *Complete Baby and Child Care* by Dr. Miriam Stoppard

A CIP catalogue record for this book is available
from the British Library
ISBN 0-7513-3614-9

Reproduced by Colourscan, Singapore
Printed and bound in the Slovak Republic
by Tlaciarne BB s.r.o., Banska Bystrica

CONTENTS

INTRODUCTION

Toddlers are at one of the most interesting and challenging stages of growing up. They are making huge strides in all areas of development and need a great deal of patience, understanding and support from their parents if they are going to realize their full potential, which is every child's birthright after all.

Toddlers' ambition outstrips their skills in almost every area, resulting in frustration, tears, tantrums, sulks and anti-social behaviour in general. They need a lot of guidance and help at this stage of their lives and parents should remember that *words* of advice are useless to a three-year-old. Actions are what they need, so you must demonstrate everything, getting down on your hands and knees to show and tell if need be.

Toddlers are always endlessly curious. Because their world is expanding so rapidly – it is virtually exploding – they want answers at every turn. And the only thing to do is to answer all of their questions – none is too trivial or too difficult – in a form they can relate to and understand.

Toddlers are also acquiring a strong sense of self and their place in the world, which is why they pit their will endlessly against yours. This apparent stubbornness is not the problem it may seem, for it offers parents the opportunity to teach valuable, lifelong lessons, for example give and take, kindness, sharing and being reasonable, helpful and kind. A good way to start most sentences to a toddler is, "Well, no. Around here we do things like this…". While parenthood may be one of the most responsible and challenging jobs around, it is also one of the most rewarding.

EVERYDAY CARE

To a spirited toddler, much of everyday care is very boring and to be avoided at all costs, but small adjustments in routine can pre-empt tantrums. Something as simple as delaying washing till after breakfast and doing everything first yourself to show her how can help to keep tempers sweet.

As your child gets older, she will gradually become more independent. By the age of four she will be able to feed, wash and dress herself and she may have strong opinions about the clothes she prefers to wear and the food she likes to eat.

GIRLS' WEIGHT

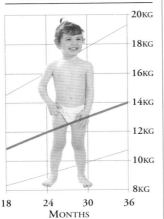

20KG
18KG
16KG
14KG
12KG
10KG
8KG

18   24   30   36
MONTHS

Weight and age charts
These two charts (see also
column, right) show the wide
ranges of weight within
which a "normal" child may
fall. The red line represents
the 50th centile: 50 per cent
of toddlers will fall below this
line and 50 per cent above.
The lines either side represent
extremes, outside which a
tiny proportion of children
will fall. If your child falls
outside the norm, talk to
your doctor.

A balanced diet
Variety is the key to a good
diet. Choose foods from each
of the groups in the chart.

TODDLER FOOD

Your child's nutritional needs increase in proportion to her
growth; she needs greater quantities during growth spurts
and when she's learning to walk. Her diet should contain
sufficient amounts of protein, carbohydrates, fats, vitamins
and minerals; she'll get all of these as long as you provide a
wide variety of foods. Because she's growing, she still needs
more protein and calories for her body weight than an adult.

NUTRIENTS PROVIDED BY DIFFERENT FOODS

FOOD GROUPS	NUTRIENTS
Breads and cereals Wholemeal bread, noodles, pasta, rice	Protein, carbohydrates, B vitamins, iron, calcium
Citrus fruits Oranges, grapefruits, lemons, limes	Vitamins A and C
Fats Butter, margarine, vegetable oils, fish oils, nut oils	Vitamins A and D, essential fatty acids
Green and yellow vegetables Cabbage, sprouts, spinach, kale, green beans, squash, lettuce, celery, courgettes	Minerals, including calcium, chlorine, fluorine, chromium, cobalt, copper, zinc, manganese, potassium, sodium and magnesium
High protein foods Chicken, fish, lamb, beef, pork, offal, eggs, cheese, nuts, legumes	Protein, fat, iron, vitamins A and D, B vitamins, especially B^{12} (naturally present in animal proteins only)
Milk and dairy products Milk, cream, yogurt, fromage frais, ice cream, cheese	Protein, fat, calcium, vitamins A and D, B vitamins
Other vegetables and fruits Potatoes, beetroot, carrots, sweetcorn, cauliflower, pineapples, apricots, nectarines, strawberries, plums, apples, bananas	Carbohydrates, vitamins A, B and C

Although, broadly speaking, a variety of carbohydrates, fruit and vegetables (fibre) and protein-rich foods will fulfil your child's needs, some foods have particular nutritional value. All fruit and vegetables provide carbohydrates and fibre, for instance, but leafy vegetables are particularly high in minerals, while citrus fruits are a good source of vitamins A and C (see chart, opposite).

PLANNING SNACKS

Snack foods should contribute to the whole day's nutrition, so don't just leave them to chance; plan them carefully, and co-ordinate meals and snacks so that you serve different foods in the snacks and in the meals.

• Milk and milk-based drinks make very good snacks, and contain protein, calcium and many of the B vitamins. You should use whole milk until your child is at least two years old; then you can use semi-skimmed but not skimmed milk unless your child is overweight (see column, p.11). Raw fruit juice drinks are also very nutritious, and rich in vitamin C. If you buy fruit juices, avoid those with added sugar.

• Your child may become bored with certain kinds of food, so try to give her plenty of variety, and make snacks amusing if you can: you could use biscuit cutters to cut cheese or bread into interesting shapes, or make a smiling face by arranging pieces of fruit on a slice of bread.

• A food that your child rejects in one form may be acceptable in another: yogurt can be frozen so that it becomes more like ice cream, and a child who rejects cheese sandwiches might enjoy eating cheese and tomato pieces out of an ice-cream cone.

• You can also increase your child's interest in food by involving her in planning or even preparing part of a snack. She will take great pride in eating a sandwich if you allow her to assemble the bread and filling herself, for example.

FAMILY EATING

It's unreasonable and very unfair to impose on a toddler an adult pattern of eating. Toddlers rarely eat "meals" as adults think of them. Nor do they need to. Snacking is much more their style. It's just as healthy as meals, but it's better for them because it maintains a stream of energy and stops them getting irritable. If you must, split all the "meals" for one day into eight or so snacks so that your toddler gets all the food *you* want in the *way* she wants.

BOYS' WEIGHT

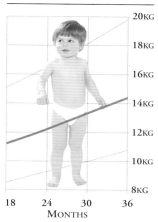

	20KG
	18KG
	16KG
	14KG
	12KG
	10KG
	8KG

18   24   30   36
MONTHS

Your toddler's weight
Your child may have spurts of growth, during which weight is quickly gained, but these will balance out with periods of slower weight gain. Any weight within the coloured band is normal.

Little and often
Your child will need more snacks than you do, since he can't eat large meals.

PORTABLE CHAIRS

Your child can eat at the table in her usual high chair, but there are other types of seat available that are more portable and will give her greater independence.

Clip-on chairs
These light, collapsible chairs are suitable for babies over six months. Some grip the table when your child sits in the chair; others are attached to the table by clamps. These are not necessarily suitable for all tables, so be sure to read the manufacturer's recommendations carefully before buying.

Booster seat
Help your child reach table height with a purpose-made seat, suitable for children over 18 months. It is more stable than a cushion, and can be strapped to a chair.

It will be some time, however, before your child is ready to sit still during mealtimes. If she wants to get down from the table, let her go, and don't try to make her come back to finish her food if she has obviously lost interest in it; she will make up for it by eating more at the next meal.

MESSY EATERS

Your child may regard mealtimes as just another game, and will see nothing wrong in getting food everywhere. Although it may seem that she is doing it on purpose, it's just a phase, and her co-ordination will improve eventually. Make mealtimes easier on yourself by surrounding the high chair with newspaper, which can be gathered up after each meal and thrown away. Being tidy can be turned into a game: you could draw a circle on the tray of the high chair to show your toddler where her mug should go; if she keeps it there, reward her.

FOOD PREFERENCES

In the second year your child will start to show likes and dislikes for certain foods. It is very common for children to go through phases of eating only one kind of food and refusing everything else. For example, she may go for a week eating nothing but yogurt and fruit, then suddenly go right off yogurt and start eating nothing but cheese and mashed potato. Don't get cross with your child about this, and don't insist that she eats certain foods. No single food is essential to your child, and there is always a nutritious substitute for any food she refuses to eat. As long as you offer your child a wide variety of foods, she will get a balanced diet, and it is far better for her to eat something that she likes – even if it's something you disapprove of – than to eat nothing at all. The one thing you must watch out for is your toddler refusing to eat any food from a particular group – refusing any kind of fruit or vegetables, for example. If she does, her diet will become unbalanced, so you will have to think of ways of tempting her to eat fruit and vegetables, perhaps by cooking the food in a different way, cutting it into shapes or presenting it to resemble a pet or favourite toy.

If you spend time cooking food that you know your toddler doesn't want, you will feel annoyed and resentful when she doesn't eat it, so give yourself and her a break by cooking food that you know she will enjoy.

FOOD INTOLERANCE AND ALLERGY

The inability to digest certain foods fully (food intolerance) has to be distinguished from a true food allergy, which is entirely different and very rare. Intolerance occurs when the digestive system fails to produce essential enzymes that break down food inside the body. One of the most

SUGGESTED "MEALS" AGE 18 MONTHS

Instead of having three meals a day and several snacks, your toddler might snack all day and that's fine. Just make sure you choose snack foods that you would have served at mealtimes. All the suggested "meals" may be mixed up.

Breakfasts
- ½ slice wholemeal toast; 1 chopped hard-boiled egg; 1 cup diluted fruit juice *or*
- 25g cereal plus ½ cup milk; 1 sliced pear, without skin; ½ slice wholemeal toast; 1 cup diluted fruit juice *or*
- 1 tablespoon baby muesli with 50ml milk; ½ mashed banana; small tub of fruit yogurt; 1 cup diluted fruit juice.

Lunches
- 50g white fish; 50g (dry weight) brown rice; 1 tablespoon sweetcorn; 1 cup diluted fruit juice *or*
- 1 beefburger in a wholemeal roll; 30g steamed broccoli; 1 medium tomato; 1 cup diluted fruit juice *or*
- 1 cheese sandwich made with wholemeal bread; pieces of raw carrot; 1 sliced apple, without skin; 1 cup milk.

Dinners
- 50–75g cauliflower with 50g grated cheese; 50g broad beans; 50g chicken pieces, without skin; ½ banana blended with 1 cup milk; 1 small wholemeal roll *or*
- ½ wholemeal roll; 50g broad beans; 50g chopped liver; 50g (dry weight) wholemeal pasta; 1 cup water *or*
- 2 sardines (not in oil); 50g baked beans; 1 medium tomato; 1 cup milk.

Snacks
- 1 small yogurt; 1 banana; 1 wholemeal bread roll; 1 cup water *or*
- 1 unsweetened wholemeal biscuit; 1 rice cake; 1 cup milk; 1 cup water *or*
- 1 orange in pieces; 1 fromage frais; 1 packet unsalted crisps; 1 cup diluted fresh fruit juice.

OVERWEIGHT

The majority of plump children are not medically overweight and no special action is needed as long as they are healthy and active.

If you think your child is overweight (that is, markedly fatter than her friends), consult your doctor who will be able to tell you if her weight is above the normal range for her height.

The commonest causes of obesity are a poor diet and lack of exercise. The best help for the child is often for the whole family to adopt a healthier diet: less fat and sugar, more fresh fruit and vegetables and more unrefined carbohydrates.

You should never aim to make your child lose weight, but for her weight to remain stable while she grows in height. The following guidelines may help:

- *Bake, grill and boil foods rather than roasting or frying.*
- *Give water or diluted fruit juice when your child is thirsty. Never give sweetened drinks.*
- *Give wholemeal bread, raw vegetables and fruit as snacks.*
- *Wholemeal bread and pasta and brown rice are more filling than refined varieties.*
- *Play lively games with your child to help her be active.*
- *No child needs more than 500ml (one pint) of milk a day. You can use skimmed or semi-skimmed cows' milk for overweight children over the age of one year if you also give vitamin supplements.*

REFUSAL TO EAT

Not eating is an early indication that your child may be unwell, so observe her carefully. If she looks pale and seems fretful and more clumsy than usual, check her temperature (see pp. 70 and 71) and speak to your doctor if you're worried.

Occasionally your child may have had a lot of snacks or a drink of milk before her meal, and she won't show her usual appetite. As long as the snacks are nutritious, this is nothing to worry about.

If your child refuses to eat for no reason that you can see, don't let yourself be bothered by it. Your child will always eat as much food as she really needs, and if you insist on her eating, mealtimes may become a battle that you will always lose.

common forms of food intolerance in children is lactose intolerance – the inability to digest the sugars in milk. The enzyme, in this case lactase, may be absent from birth, or its production may be disrupted by an intestinal disorder such as gastroenteritis. Pale-coloured, bulky, smelly stools are characteristic of the disorder.

Most cases of suspected food allergy turn out to be no more than intolerance, or the combination of a fussy child and a fussy mother. A true food allergy is quite rare, and occurs when the body's immune system over-reacts to a food it interprets as "foreign". It is a protective mechanism and symptoms can include headache, nausea, profuse vomiting, a rash, widespread red blotches on the skin, and swelling of the mouth, tongue, face and eyes. Wheat, shellfish, strawberries, chocolate, eggs and cows' milk are the foods most likely to cause allergic reactions.

In the 1980s, food allergies attracted a great deal of attention, and were blamed for behavioural disturbances in children, including hyperactivity. More recent studies have cast doubt on these claims: parents continued to report behavioural disturbance even when, unknown to them, the suspect food had been withdrawn from the child's diet. In a very small number of cases it has been proved that food was responsible for the behaviour, but in very many more cases bad behaviour is a way of seeking love and attention from neglectful parents. I feel very strongly that too many parents have been willing to blame foods for behavioural problems rather than look to their own attitudes as a cause, needlessly depriving many children of nutritious foods. You should never attempt to isolate a food allergy on your own without medical advice, and never assume an allergy is present without a clear diagnosis from a paediatric allergist.

FAMILY AND SOCIAL EATING

Your older toddler will eat broadly the same diet as you, and her dietary needs should be seen in the context of the eating habits of the whole family; you may even have taken the opportunity to improve your own diet as a result of considering the needs of your child. At this stage, you will probably be concerned less about making sure your child is getting the right foods in the right amounts, and more about whether she is learning adult behaviour and manners at mealtimes. This is a good time to teach her table manners that will last into adulthood.

For many families, mealtimes are about much more than making sure everyone is fed; they are social occasions when all the members of the family sit down together, exchange news, and enjoy each other's company. For a small child, these times form an important part of her learning process; she can appreciate this social aspect of mealtimes and will learn most of her behaviour at table from her experience of family eating, rather than from any number of lectures at a later age. Every family has its own accepted standards of behaviour and I am not going to lay down rules about what these should be. What is important, however, is that your child learns to fit in so that the family can enjoy their mealtimes together without repeated disruptions caused by bad manners and arguments about behaviour.

From the time your child first sat in her high chair at the family dining table, she has been watching and learning. She will want at least to try the foods that you are eating and will often join in the conversation. Try to include your child in family meals as often as possible. Encourage her when she attempts to follow your (good) example. Give praise, for instance, when she asks for something to be passed to her instead of attempting to grab it from the other side of the table. Children learn most naturally and easily by example and will rapidly pick up the norms of behaviour that the rest of the family observe. If yours is a family where everyone leaves the table when it suits them, for example, rather than waiting for the others to finish eating, it will be hard to persuade your child to sit still and wait until everyone is finished.

KEEPING MEALTIMES RELAXED

It is important to prevent mealtimes from becoming a battleground. If you're insistent and authoritarian, your toddler will soon start to use food as a weapon in a war she will always win. In the end you can't force her to eat, so be cool and conciliatory at mealtimes, knowing there's no such thing as an essential food. If you don't adopt this attitude, your child may see food as a weapon that she uses to gain attention or to express anger, distress and many other emotions. It is best, therefore, to be fairly easy-going about table etiquette with your child, to make mealtimes as relaxed as possible and not to be drawn into arguments. Insist only on table manners that you consider absolutely essential; refinements can come later.

EATING OUT

Your child will have definite preferences about what she wants to eat. As she grows older there are likely to be more occasions when she is eating away from home, and while you can't account for every mouthful she eats, you should try to ensure that the good habits she has learned at home are not undermined once she starts to eat out.

If your child goes out to playgroup, nursery school or "proper" school, try to make sure she has a good breakfast before she goes. If she doesn't, she will get hungry again long before lunchtime, and both her temper and her concentration will be affected. A healthy mid-morning snack like a piece of fruit or cereal bar will help tide her over until lunchtime.

If lunch is going to be provided, try to find out what will be on offer; if you are not satisfied, or if there are no arrangements to feed your child, then provide her with a nutritious packed lunch instead. Lunch need not always be sandwiches; you could give chicken pieces and potato salad, pieces of raw vegetables with a yogurt dip, or other foods that your child can eat with her fingers.

Children are often encouraged to try new foods because they see their friends eat them; you may find when your child starts at playgroup or school, she starts to eat foods that she previously rejected at home.

BATHROOM
SAFETY

*Baths should be carefully
supervised since a toddler is
still at risk from slipping and
falling under the water.
Remember to follow these
safety guidelines:*

• *Place a non-slip bath mat
in the bottom of the bath.*

• *Check the temperature of the
water before putting your child
in the bath. Even for toddlers,
it needs to be considerably
cooler than for most adults.*

• *Turn off the taps tightly
before putting your toddler
in the bath.*

• *When you lift your toddler
out of the bath, make sure that
you are standing steadily. Take
the strain with your legs, not
your back.*

• *Toddlers are generally keen
to do things for themselves –
washing their own face, for
example – so there is the risk
that your child may turn on
the hot tap or grab the soap or
shampoo and get it in her eyes.
Covering the taps with a towel
is a good way to soften any
bangs or falls.*

• *A child who has previously
been happy in the bath may
take against it, especially if she
gets a fright while bathing – for
instance, if she falls over or
bangs herself. Providing lots of
amusements in the bath, and
perhaps getting her to share the
bath with a sibling, can help
reduce this problem. Allowing
her to share a bath with you
will resolve most difficulties.*

BATHING AND HYGIENE

Your toddler will probably regard bathtime primarily as
playtime; you can take advantage of this by making a game
of teaching her how to wash herself. Let her have her own
special sponge for bathtime and show her how to wash her
face first, then her arms and legs and so on. She won't be
able to make a very good job of it yet, so you'll probably
have to go over the same areas yourself with another sponge
or facecloth. Soap your child's hands and show her how to
spread the soap over her body and arms; then make a game
of rinsing off all the suds.

WASHING ROUTINES

A child is often hungry when she wakes up, so it's best to
leave washing until after breakfast, when your child will be
more willing to stand still to have her face and hands
washed, teeth brushed (see opposite) and hair combed.
From the age of about 18 months she can start learning to
rinse her hands under running water and, later on, she will
learn to soap them, although she may make quite a mess
with the soap and water.

CLEANLINESS

The younger you start teaching hygiene the better, and the
best way of teaching is by example. Wash your hands with
your child: get your hands soapy together and wash each
other's hands, then inspect each other's hands to see whose
are the cleanest. If she finds the facecloth rough, let her use
a sponge, which is softer.

Make it clear that hands should always be washed after
using the lavatory. You should start this at the potty stage
(see p. 20) and do it with your child every single time.
Similarly, make sure your child washes her hands before
meals or after handling pets.

Encourage your child to do this for herself. Make sure
she can reach the washbasin and toilet easily by putting a
step in the bathroom for her to use, and make sure that she
knows which is the hot tap and which is the cold.

HAIR CARE

Your child will probably have a thick head of hair by now,
and this will need regular washing to remove everyday
grime. Unfortunately there are few children who enjoy this

process. You can make washing as easy as possible for your child by using the following tips to help to reduce the potential for conflict.

• Keep your child's hair short; it will be easier to brush, too.
• Use a non-sting baby shampoo and get a special halo-like shield (see p. 16) that will keep the water and suds away from her eyes.
• If your child really hates hair washing, try allowing her some control over it: choosing whether she holds her head back or forwards for washing, for example, or holding the shower and wetting her own hair.

TOOTHCARE

You will have been brushing your child's teeth from the time that they first appeared and you should continue to do so at least twice a day. Always brush your child's teeth after the evening meal so that food particles are not left in her mouth overnight. As your toddler gets older, she will probably want to hold the toothbrush and do it herself. While this should be encouraged, she will not be able to clean her own teeth effectively, and you should always follow up her efforts yourself with a thorough brushing.

When brushing your child's teeth, use a small, soft-bristled brush and a toothpaste containing fluoride. Sit your child sideways on your knee, holding her securely with one arm, and gently brush the teeth up and down. If she won't keep her head still, try gently resting your free hand on her forehead.

With any luck it will be years before your toddler will need any form of dental treatment. Nonetheless, it is important to get her used to the idea of going to the dentist. Make a point of taking her with you when you go for a check-up. Most dentists are sympathetic and like to remove any possibility of fear in young patients. He or she will probably be happy for your child to sit in the "magic" chair and will ask her to open her mouth so that her teeth can be checked and counted.

NAILS

Keep your child's fingernails and toenails cut short; use blunt-ended scissors, specially designed to be safe for young children, or nail clippers. You will find it easier to restrain your wriggling child if you sit her on your lap. Follow the natural line of her fingernails and do not cut too close to the quick. Toenails should be cut straight across.

PETS AND HYGIENE

You may be concerned about the possible health risks to your toddler in having a pet. However, if you follow a few simple rules of hygiene, you should have no cause for concern, and the rewards to your child will be well worth the effort.

• *Ringworm (see p. 17) is a contagious skin condition that can be caught from pets, and it is common in children. If you suspect ringworm, see your doctor straight away.*

• *Always try to stop your child kissing her pet, especially near its nose and mouth.*

• *Encourage your child to wash her hands after playing with her pet – especially before touching or eating food.*

• *Both fleas and worms are easily avoided by regular use of preventive treatments. Consult your vet if necessary.*

• *If infestation occurs, treat it promptly and keep your child away from any pets until the treatment has worked.*

CLEANLINESS IN GIRLS

Most girls are naturally fastidious, and you can take advantage of this in teaching your child how to wash and keep herself clean.

• *Encourage good habits in your little girl from an early age by showing her how to wash herself and clean her teeth (see Toothcare, p. 15).*

• *Let her brush her own hair; she will prefer it, and it means she can choose her own hairstyle, ribbons, slides or hairband.*

• *Let her have her own special facecloth, soap dish and towel; she'll be proud of her own things in the bathroom.*

• *Allow her to rub baby lotion into her skin after bathing.*

• *Teach her to change her underwear and socks daily.*

• *Provide her own laundry basket so that she can discard her own dirty clothes.*

OLDER TODDLERS

By the time a child has reached the age of three years, she will have developed her own views on many aspects of her day-to-day life and will want to have increasing control over her daily routine. This is often expressed negatively in a reluctance or even refusal to co-operate with mundane tasks such as bathing and hairbrushing, which are often seen as unwelcome interruptions to more exciting forms of activity and play. The best way to avoid arguments is to turn washing and brushing into a game, or incorporate a fun element into the task. Allowing your child to take increasing responsibility for carrying out a task, supervised if necessary, or giving her some element of choice about the activity – choosing which comb or which shampoo to use, for example – can make it more interesting and encourage her to co-operate. The following hints will make the daily routine easier and more enjoyable for both of you:

• Try not to rush your child to complete a task she is trying to manage by herself. It leads to tension, and may make her less willing to help next time.
• Don't leave bathtime until last thing before bedtime, or your child may be too tired to enjoy it.
• Encourage interest in toothbrushing by using disclosing tablets once a week. The need to brush away the colour is a great way to ensure that your child cleans her teeth really well.
• Make hair washing fun by letting your child see in a mirror all the silly hairstyles she can create from lathered hair.

Soapy hair can be moulded to create amusing hairstyles

Hair shield
Keep soap and water off your child's face with a specially designed shield.

Make hair washing fun
Allow your child to play games to help get over a dislike of hair washing.

• Offer the bribe of the use of some "special" grown-up toiletries, such as mildly perfumed soap or bubble bath, in return for her co-operation at bathtime – I believe in bribes for young children.

EXPLAINING ABOUT HYGIENE

By the age of three your child is capable of understanding and reasoning why something is important. If you give her a reason why she shouldn't do something rather than pulling rank, she's likely to stop doing it; you'll gain her co-operation more readily if you present arguments in favour of certain actions. Explain to your child that if her hands are dirty they're covered in germs that could make her ill; that if she's eaten a sweet it could give her toothache; or that if she's handled the dog she might have germs on her hands that could give her a tummy ache.

Once your child begins to understand the reasons for washing and toothbrushing, be consistent. Children are very logical, and she will probably question you if you overlook these daily actions.

CONDITIONS PASSED BETWEEN CHILDREN

As soon as your child starts to socialize with other children, she is at risk from a variety of minor disorders that are commonly passed between children. Don't be unduly upset by these; they are not necessarily a result of poor hygiene, and can all be easily treated.

Ringworm A fungal infection affecting the scalp (*tinea capitis*) or the body (*tinea corporis*), ringworm appears as small, bald, scaly patches on the scalp or skin. These are usually oval in shape and the edges of the patch remain scaly while the centre clears, leaving rings. Consult your doctor, since the condition is irritating and contagious.

Nits (head lice) The insects themselves are difficult to see and most people first notice the pale oval-shaped eggs that become firmly attached to the hair. There are special shampoos available to treat nits, or you can wash the hair with ordinary shampoo, then soak it in plenty of conditioner and comb it through with a nit comb. If you find lice or nits, repeat this process four times over the next two weeks.

Threadworms Threadworms are the most common form of intestinal worm in the UK. They live in the bowel and lay eggs around the anus that cause the characteristic night-time anal itching. Your doctor can prescribe a treatment.

CLEANLINESS IN BOYS

Boys are usually quite resistant to washing, and you'll have to spend a lot of time reminding your little boy to wash and brush.

• *Make bathtimes as much fun as possible, with toys, games and lots of suds.*

• *Spend some time showing him how to wash, and do this several times if necessary.*

• *Try not to be over fussy about cleanliness; if he's right in the middle of a game, for example, let handwashing wait until he's ready to stop.*

• *Let him wash himself as soon as he can make an attempt, then clean him well yourself at the last moment.*

• *Encourage a daily change of underpants and socks.*

• *Give him his own laundry basket and encourage him to use it every night.*

Your little girl will try to dress herself now, so choose clothes that she can manage easily. She's growing fast, too, so don't spend a lot on clothes that she'll quickly outgrow.

• *Buy dresses with fastenings at the front; ones that fasten at the back are too difficult for your little girl to manage.*

• *Show her how to get her tights the right way round, and how to roll each leg down to the ankle before she tries to put on the tights.*

• *It's best to avoid very fitted clothes; they don't leave much room for growth.*

Room to grow
Loose-fitting clothes with adjustable fastenings are best for your child now that she's growing fast.

CLOTHES AND DRESSING

As your child grows older, she'll develop the co-ordination required to dress herself successfully. You should encourage her in her attempts at dressing or undressing, however slow or awkward – they're a sign of growing independence and increasing maturity.

At 18 months she will already be trying to manage fastenings, and by two-and-a-half she will be able to close a button in a loose buttonhole and put on her own pants, T-shirt and sweatshirt. By the age of four she will probably be able to dress or undress herself completely and will have enough dexterity to put her clothes away tidily. There are several things you can do to make getting dressed easier for your child.

• Teach her how to button from the bottom upwards.
• Sew large buttons on to a toddler's clothes so that she can handle them easily.
• Velcro fastenings will be easy for her to manage, but don't use them where they might chafe her skin.
• Buy trousers with elasticated waists instead of fiddly zip fasteners, which may catch as they're closed.
• Children find it difficult to put sweaters on the right way round, so explain to her that the label always goes at the back.

CHOOSING SHOES

The assistant should measure the length and the width of your child's foot before your child tries any shoes. Once your child tries on a pair of shoes, the assistant should press the joints of the foot to make sure that they're not restricted in any way, and he should check that the fastenings hold the shoe firmly in place and don't let your child's foot slip about. Make sure your child stands up and walks about in the shoes to check that they don't pinch her toes and hurt when she's walking, and to double-check that there's no slipping.

A sturdy, well-made pair of leather shoes is most suitable for general outdoor wear, especially once your child is running about and playing. You should, however, get a pair of Wellington boots for use in wet or muddy conditions. Although leather shoes and sandals are solid and sensible and last well, there is nothing wrong with inexpensive canvas shoes or sneakers, as long as you make sure that they fit properly.

CHOOSING CLOTHES

As your child becomes more involved in dressing herself, she will become more conscious of the clothes themselves. Babies are largely unaware of what they are wearing as long as it is comfortable and does not impede their activities, but toddlers gradually begin to notice the colours and type of clothing they put on, and your child may develop definite preferences. Clothes that seem similar to those worn by mummy or daddy might seem especially attractive. The feel of a garment will also be important to her – whether, for example, it is soft or itchy, tight or stretchy. If she takes a dislike to a garment, it may be because it doesn't fit properly and is therefore uncomfortable to wear.

Allowing your child to choose which clothes to wear each day is also important; for instance, on a cold day you may want her to wear trousers, but let her choose which pair. She may develop seemingly irrational likes or dislikes for certain items of clothing – insisting on wearing a particular T-shirt every day, for example, or refusing to wear the hand-knitted pullover that granny gave her for her birthday. The easiest policy is to go along with these preferences as far as possible, although occasionally bribery, or at least negotiation, may be in order: you could offer a special treat in return for wearing that pullover on the afternoon that granny comes to tea.

Choosing fastenings

Until your child has enough dexterity to manage fiddly buttons and zips, you need to choose clothes and shoes with manageable fastenings.

Sliding buckles can be adjusted for the best fit

Hooks are easier to manage than buttonholes

DRESSING A BOY

Help your little boy to dress himself by making sure that his clothes don't have tricky fastenings. Although it may take him quite a long time, allow him his independence, and don't step in to help unless you're really needed.

• *Boys are usually slower than girls at learning to use the potty, so it is very important to avoid awkward fastenings on your little boy's trousers.*

• *Trousers with elasticated waists are easiest but, if he has trousers with zip fasteners, show him how to pull the zip away from him as he closes it to prevent it catching.*

• *A zip fastener is easier to grasp if it has a ring attached to the tab.*

• *Show your little boy how to sit down to put his feet into his trouser legs, then stand up to pull them up.*

• *Look for adjustable straps on dungarees, or add buttons so that straps can be lengthened.*

Shoes

Velcro fastenings rather than laces or buckles will allow your child to fasten her own shoes very easily.

Teach your little girl good habits of hygiene, like washing her hands and tidying the bathroom after her. You'll probably find that she responds well to this.

Girls are generally neater than boys, and will enjoy turning a cleanliness routine into a game: "Now we flush the loo … Now we wash the potty … Now we wash our hands".

Toilet hygiene
Girls are generally more receptive than boys to being taught good habits of hygiene.

BOWEL AND BLADDER

Potty training has no place in toddler care: it simply doesn't work. It causes unhappiness in a child who's unready and it's unnecessary in a child who is ready. By all means let your baby get familiar with a potty as a toy, but nothing more until she alerts you to the fact that she can *feel* she's passing urine. Always take your lead from her, never before.

Although a baby is aware first of her bladder emptying, she will probably achieve bowel control first because it's much easier to "hold on" with a full rectum than with a full bladder. You should, therefore, help your child to use the potty for bowel movements first; this is easier, in any case, because bowel movements are more predictable and take longer than passing urine. When your child indicates that she wants to pass a stool, suggest that she use the potty, but stay cool if she doesn't want to.

BLADDER CONTROL

The first sign that your child's bladder control is developing is when she becomes aware of the passage of urine, and she may try to attract your attention and point to her nappy. As her bladder matures and is able to contain urine for longer, you may find that her nappy is dry after a nap. Once this is happening regularly, you can leave off the nappy during the nap and encourage her to empty her bladder beforehand. When she can do this and can let you know when she wants to use the potty, you can start leaving off nappies completely during the day, provided she is able to "hold on" for a few minutes while you take down her clothes to let her use the potty. When you are out, you might find it useful to carry a portable potty; these come with disposable liners.

ACHIEVING NIGHT-TIME CONTROL

Control of the bladder during the night is the last to come, since a child of two or three can't hold on to urine for much more than four to five hours. Once your child wakes up regularly with a dry nappy, you can leave off the night-time nappy, but encourage her to empty her bladder before she goes to sleep. It is a good idea to keep a potty beside the bed for your child to use if necessary, but make sure that her nightclothes are easy for her to take down and that you leave a night-light on so that she can see what she's doing.

HOW TO HELP A YOUNG TODDLER

Do ...

• Praise your child and encourage her to regard bowel and bladder control as an accomplishment.
• Let your child set the pace. You can help your child along, but you can't speed up the process.
• Suggest that your child sits on the potty, but allow her to make the decision.
• Let your child be as independent as she likes, going to the lavatory or using the potty, and praise her independence.
• Use trainer pants (see p. 22) to give your child a sense of independence.

Don't ...

• Insist that your child sit on the potty, ever.
• Show any disgust for your child's faeces. She will regard using the potty as an achievement and will be proud of them.
• Ask your child to wait once she has asked for the potty, even for a moment; she can "hold on" only for a very short time.
• Scold mistakes and accidents.

AIDING A BOY

Boys are often messier than girls in using the potty or the toilet, but there are some things that you can do to help your little boy.

Show your little boy how to stand in front of the lavatory and teach him to aim at the bowl before he passes any urine. You could put a piece of toilet paper in the bowl for him to aim at. Let him see his father passing urine so that he can imitate him.

Boys are more likely than girls to play with their faeces. If this happens, don't show disgust; just wash your child's hands calmly, as you would if they were dirty with mud or paint.

If she does show signs of becoming more self-reliant, encourage her and boost her confidence. She will still have accidents, so it is a good idea to protect the mattress with a rubber sheet, putting your usual sheet on top. You could also put a small rubber sheet on top of the ordinary one, with a half sheet over that. The half sheet can then be easily removed after an accident, and the undersheet will be protected by the rubber sheet.

USING THE LAVATORY

When your child starts using the potty regularly throughout the day, encourage her to sit on the lavatory; this will save you having to take a potty with you when you leave the house. Many children are nervous of sitting on the lavatory seat because they feel they'll fall off or even fall in. To make your child more secure on the large lavatory seat, you can use one of the specially designed child-sized seats available that fit inside the lavatory rim. Suggest that she holds on to the sides so she feels balanced. You should also stay near by until you are quite sure that she is comfortable on the seat. To help her to get up easily, put a small step or box in front of the lavatory; she can also use this to reach the handbasin.

Potties
Specially moulded potties provide support and are suitable for both boys and girls.

TRAINER PANTS

Before your child's bladder control is fully developed you may like to use trainer pants. She will probably prefer them to nappies because they seem more grown up.

• *Disposable trainer pants have easily tearable side seams so that they can be quickly removed in case of accidents.*

• *Non-disposable trainer pants are more absorbent than the disposable kind and can therefore be left on at night. They are also more bulky, however, so some children find them uncomfortable.*

OLDER TODDLERS

By three years of age most children have fairly reliable bladder and bowel control, but accidents will still be common. During the day accidents are most likely to happen when your child ignores the signals of a full bladder because she is engrossed in play or because she is reluctant to use the lavatory in an unfamiliar place. You can help by reminding your child to go to the lavatory at regular intervals and by making a point of accompanying her to the lavatory when you visit new surroundings. In familiar places, encourage your child to go independently as soon as possible, but never insist on her going to a strange lavatory alone.

Some children achieve bowel and bladder control later because brain–bladder connections take longer than average to form, so it is wrong and cruel to blame your child. Lateness in acquiring control is often hereditary; ask your parents and parents-in-law about this.

ACCIDENTS AND BEDWETTING

When your child does wet herself, remember that however badly you may feel about the inconvenience, it's likely that her embarrassment is much worse. Reassure her that you understand it was an accident and that she hasn't failed you. Being prepared for accidents will reduce anxiety for both of you; always carry spare underwear and trousers on outings.

Bedwetting at night (see p. 20) can happen to a child of any age. It is very common in children up to the age of five, boys being especially prone. Most children grow out of it after this age without any special help.

You will minimize your child's embarrassment if you keep her in nappies at night until you are confident that she has reached the point where she can stay dry all night. Once you let her go without nappies, be prepared for the occasional accident. Concern about the frequency of bedwetting should not be communicated to your child; it only increases her anxiety. Encourage her instead by giving special praise if she has a dry night.

CONSTIPATION

Constipation without any other signs of illness is nothing to worry about, but if it causes your child discomfort, consult your doctor. You should never try to treat constipation yourself with laxatives, suppositories or enemas.

Once your child is on a varied diet, she shouldn't suffer from constipation if you are giving her enough fresh fruit, vegetables and wholemeal breads; if she does, just give more of these foods. The complex carbohydrates in root and green vegetables contain cellulose, which holds water in the stools and makes them more bulky and soft, as do oat cereals like porridge. A few stewed prunes or dried figs can help, too, often producing a soft stool within 24 hours.

A child can become chronically constipated for several reasons: if you are an over-fussy parent and obsessive about the frequency of her bowel movements, your child may withhold them as a means of getting attention; if she has experienced pain and discomfort when trying to pass a motion, she may hold on to the stools to prevent the pain from recurring; or if she dislikes school or other strange lavatories and is unwilling to use them.

Illness with a high temperature may be followed by a few days of constipation, partly because your child has eaten very little, so there are no waste products to pass, and partly because she has lost water through sweating with the fever. This kind of constipation will correct itself when your child goes back on to a normal diet.

HOW TO HELP AN OLDER TODDLER

Do ...	Don't ...
• Remind your child to go to the lavatory at regular intervals.	• Scold or draw attention to any form of accident your child has.
• Take a spare set of clothes with you when you go out.	• Withhold fluids from your child in the evening.
• Accompany your child to the lavatory in unfamiliar places to reassure her.	• Compare your child with others of the same age who may have better control.
• Be sympathetic and make light of any accidents.	• Make an issue out of any accident in front of friends.
• Offer praise when your child has a dry night.	• Be unsympathetic if your child needs to use the toilet at an inconvenient moment.
• Look for the cause within the family first if wetting or soiling occurs after a long period of reliable control. If it persists, seek advice from your doctor.	

REGRESSION

In a child who has been reliably dry for some time, regression to night- or day-time wetting is usually a sign of anxiety.

The arrival of a new baby is a typical reason for your child regressing to an earlier stage as a way of winning back your attention, but any sort of upset such as a move to a new home or school can cause it.

Occasionally, regression can be caused by an infection of the urinary tract, so when you visit the doctor for any urinary problem, take a sample of your child's urine for testing.

Bowel control, once developed, is usually much more reliable than bladder control. Bowel accidents are uncommon and, if they occur frequently, particularly after control has apparently been reliable for some time, may indicate an underlying problem such as retention of stool or some form of emotional tension. Seek advice from your doctor.

INJURIES

Toddlers tend to cry at even the most minor injury such as a small scratch, an abrasion or a tiny bruise.

In our house, I always had the "magic cream" (a mild, antiseptic cream) on hand, and my children responded almost at once to attention, reassurance and a thin smear of the "magic cream". Sometimes I had to sit down with them, hold them close, give them a big cuddle and make very sympathetic sounds to show them that I knew how much it was hurting or how frightened they were – many young children are terrified by the sight of blood. Comfort and the "magic cream" nearly always had a calming effect.

Whenever your child comes to you in distress, crying over a small injury, be sympathetic. Say you know how much it's hurting and don't try to make her be brave. In a few moments she'll skip off your knee and return to her play after a kiss to make it better, a cuddle and a favourite drink or snack.

If necessary, put some interesting idea into your child's mind to distract her from the injury, such as a special treat for tea, a special game with dad, a picnic, or an outing to a favourite place.

WHEN YOUR TODDLER CRIES

Emotionally, your toddler is developing very rapidly. She can feel guilt, shame, jealousy and dislike, and be so upset that these emotions make her cry. Her fears are related to daytime activities and any upset arising from them.

DEALING WITH FEARS

The commonest fears in this age group are of the dark and of thunder. One of the best ways to dispel fears is to talk about them, so encourage your child to be open and frank about what frightens her. Give her your full attention and ask questions, so that she knows that you are taking her seriously. Quite often fears are difficult to put into words, but hear your child out. Help her to explain by supplying a few examples, and confess that you have similar fears too. Never scold or ridicule your child about her fears. Do something simple and reassuring, like demonstrating to your child that it is fun in the swimming pool and the water is nothing to fear. Your child will trust you and her fear will gradually diminish. When she's old enough, try to explain how things work: for instance, that lightning is just like a giant spark of light.

FEAR OF SEPARATION

Even when your child is three years old, she will still have fears about losing you. When she was younger, she worried about losing sight of you; now, she is fearful that you will not come back, that you will die while you are away from her and that she will be deprived of you forever. Again, a very good way to reassure your child is to go step by step through what is going to happen when you leave her. The more details you can give, and the more you can confirm the details, the better.

A NEW BABY

Your child is bound to feel pretty distressed at the thought of a new baby brother or sister and the "dethronement" that she thinks will follow. Take all the precautions you can to make her feel good about the baby. When you talk about the baby, refer to her as the new sister or brother, and let your child feel your tummy as the baby grows and kicks.

Show her where the baby is going to sleep, and teach her all kinds of helpful things she can do to look after her. If you are having the baby in hospital, make sure your child is at ease with the person who is going to look after her while you're there. When you come home, have someone else carry the baby; you should have your arms free to scoop up your child and give her a big cuddle. Don't turn to the new baby until she asks to see her. Make sure that you bring home a present from the baby for her. If you have to stay in hospital, let her visit you as often as she likes, and when she does, make sure that the baby is not in your arms, but is lying in a cot at your side so you're free to hold your child.

OVER-TIREDNESS

A child of this age very often becomes over-excited and over-tired towards bedtime. She'll try to put off her bedtime as long as possible, and simply become more distressed. Your child might become so fragile that any small discomfort or frustration will make her cry inconsolably.

If you are expecting your child to have a late evening or a special treat such as a party or a school play, make sure she has a nap during the day so that her energy will last. If she does become over-excited and over-tired, it is especially important that you remain calm and quiet. Talk to her gently, give her lots of cuddles, be infinitely patient and take her gently to her bedroom. Sing her a song or read a story until she has become calm and quietened down.

Fearful toddler
Always take your child's fears seriously and ask her to explain them if she can.

TANTRUMS

Toddlers between the ages of two and three often have temper tantrums as a means of giving vent to frustration when they do not get what they want.

This is quite normal because your child will not have sufficient judgment to control her strength of will or the language to express herself clearly, but as her knowledge and experience of the world broadens, so the occasions when her will is pitched directly against yours become less frequent.

A tantrum may be brought on by such feelings as frustration, anger, jealousy and dislike. Anger is brought on by not getting her own way; frustration by her not being sufficiently strong or well co-ordinated to do what she wants. The tantrum will usually involve your child throwing herself on the floor, kicking and screaming.

The best thing you can do is to stay calm, since any attention on your part will only prolong the attack. If she has a one in public, take her to a quiet place, without fuss.

At home, an effective technique is simply to leave the room. Explain to your child that, while you still love her, you have to leave the room because you are getting angry. Never confine her in another room because this denies her the option of coming back and saying sorry.

LIFTING YOUR TODDLER

Make sure you know how to handle your toddler or other heavy weights in a way that won't strain your back.

Once you have a baby, there are many opportunities for putting a strain on your back. Your child requires constant lifting and carrying, and prams, pushchairs and other equipment must be shifted. It's important that you learn to lift without injury and strain. Keep your back straight, bend your knees and, using the powerful thigh muscles to do all the work, lift. Never lift with your legs straight and your back curved forward.

SHARING WITH OTHER CHILDREN

Young children are naturally selfish and usually begin to think of others only when they're taught to do so. Your child has to understand that other children feel as she does before she is able to grasp the importance of thinking of other people's feelings. Do not worry if your child seems to be slow in learning to share; it's very difficult, but with your patience she will successfully acquire this skill.

HOLDING AND HANDLING

Never refuse your toddler a cuddle; although she will need less holding than when she was a young baby, she will often ask to be carried like she used to when she's been out for a long walk, or when she's generally tired and cranky. She's likely to be clingy when she feels pain or discomfort, when a tooth is coming through or if she is feeling off colour. You should always respond to her signals and not hesitate to give her a hug for comfort and affection. Your child will soon make it clear when she has had enough reassurance, and will get down and run off. Babies who are given love and cuddles when they need and ask for them usually grow into independent and self-confident individuals.

The desire for physical affection remains with us always. Parents should never scoff at their children's needs, and should always respond to them. When my children were growing up, they liked a cuddle every now and then, especially when they were tired, had had a telling-off from a teacher at school, if they were fearful about my departure or absence, or if the world simply didn't feel right.

"CLINGY" CHILDREN

Older children will still occasionally want to sit on your lap. When they feel ill at ease in strange circumstances, they may even want to eat sitting on your knee, particularly if strangers are present and they feel that they are being watched. Let them do so if it is convenient; you will find that just a few moments of intimacy will give a child the confidence to handle any situation.

Bedtimes are particularly important times for showing affection. In my opinion, a child should never have to go to bed without some cuddling. A cuddle will provide a sense of security and the conviction that you really do care. The rule is that you should always be there with a comforting arm and a kind word when your child is hurt, worried, puzzled or frightened. Not all children require physical reassurance, so be prepared to provide comfort in the form that your child wants.

SHOWING AFFECTION

By the age of three or four years, your child will be much more independent, and you may assume that she needs fewer overt displays of affection. While this may be true, it would be a mistake to think that she wants to go without any physical affection at all. You should pay special attention to boys, who are often expected to give up cuddles and kisses at a very young age because it is not considered to be proper "masculine" behaviour.

It is all too easy to lose the habit of showing affection, so make a resolution to hold and touch your child as often as you can every day, whether it's letting her sit on your knee or putting an arm around her when you look at the paper, or giving her a cuddle when you put her to bed. I made it a rule to tell my children every day that I loved them.

DIVIDING YOUR ATTENTION

It can be very difficult to divide your time and attention evenly between several young children. A friend of mine, who had twins, adopted a pragmatic approach to this problem: rather than trying to give each twin an equal share of her attention at all times, she decided to attend to whichever twin needed her at any one time, and assumed that it would all even out over the years.

Her example is a good one to follow; for much of the time you will give your children equal attention, so if one of them demands more, you should feel free to give it.

COMFORT AND ENCOURAGEMENT

With any luck your child won't be averse to a cuddle even after she's reached adulthood, but cuddles do change and get more grown-up, and you have to give the kind of cuddles your child needs rather than the kind you want to give. So adapt your style of cuddling to what gives her most comfort.

Preschool children need plenty of cuddles every day, especially congratulatory ones, for instance when they've mastered something like getting their shoes on the right feet. Comfort cuddles are essential at the first sign of tears. A child responds much better to a cuddle than a reprimand.

THERAPEUTIC CUDDLES

Many of your child's troubles can be solved with a hug and a few sympathetic words.

Therapeutic cuddles reduce the pain of a prick, a knock or a cut (even a big one) in seconds.

Never let your child go to sleep without a huge hug and an "I love you".

As your child gets older, cuddles are transformed into other actions, but have the same bolstering effect. A hand on the shoulder, a small caress, or just taking your child's hand as a sign of love will make her self-esteem and confidence soar.

Your child craves your love and approval; never leave her in any doubt that she has both in full measure.

*To help your child make the
switch to a big bed, recreate a
secure environment like the
one she had in her cot.*

*Tell your child that now she's a
big girl, she's very lucky to get
to sleep in a big bed "like
mummy and daddy do".*

*Put lots of her favourite toys
in her new bed and consider
installing a night-light or just
leaving the bedroom door open
so she can see the landing light.*

*If music helps to soothe her,
leave a favourite tape or CD
playing while she goes to sleep.*

*Once you've put your child to
bed, don't make the mistake of
disappearing suddenly, since
this will unsettle her. Instead,
make sure she is comfortable:
sing songs or read a story, leave
a drink by the bed (and a
potty if necessary), and then
say goodnight more than once
without closing the door so she
knows you're still there.*

SLEEP AND WAKEFULNESS

Many two-year-olds periodically wake up during the night.
If your child is one of them, this may be distressing for you
and your partner, but it is both usual and normal, and you
should never deny your child love, comfort and affection.
There may be some obvious problem for your child's
waking up, but often you won't be able to find out a reason
for this happening. It could just be that she's a bit afraid of
the dark, but she cannot explain to you what is wrong, nor
can you reassure her with words. You have to comfort her
with actions, so give lots of kisses and cuddles to show your
child that she is loved.

Daytime naps As your child gets older you will find that
she doesn't necessarily want to sleep at nap time, but she
still does need a rest. Try to make a routine out of nap time
whether your child sleeps or not by, say, playing some
music or reading. You may find your child goes to sleep at
nap time if you allow her to sleep in your bed as a special
treat, or if you give her some idea of how long the nap time
will be; one way of doing this is to put on her favourite tape
and say that nap time isn't over until the tape is finished.

FROM COT TO BED

When your child is strong enough and well co-ordinated
enough to climb out of her cot and come into your room,
it is time for her to start using a bed. Most children will be
pleased and excited with their new bed, but if your child
seems nervous, there are plenty of things you can do to help

Day-time naps
During the day watch your child for signs
of bad temper or fretfulness and ensure
that she rests or plays a quiet game.

(see column, left); the simplest is to let her take naps in the bed until she is ready to sleep in it at night. If you are worried that your child might fall out of the bed, you could fit a bed guard to one or both sides as appropriate.

PLEASANT BEDTIMES

From the age of three onwards, your child may well use delaying tactics in order to put off going to bed. The way you handle this situation really depends on how much energy you have at the end of the day, and what your previous bedtime routine has been.

If you've been looking after your child and managing the household tasks all day, you will be in need of private time and may feel you can insist on her going to bed. On the other hand, if you have been out at work all day, you will want to see your child, so you may feel very sympathetic to her pleas for your attention.

If you've always had quite a strict bedtime routine and your child suddenly departs from this, then it's probably best for both of you if you firmly re-institute the bedtime with loving fairness. If, however, you've always been flexible about bedtimes, then it's probably as well for your child's happiness and peace of mind and your serenity to let her stay with you and make herself comfortable. She will be asleep in a few minutes if she has the reassurance of your presence in the room.

KEEPING BEDTIME PEACEFUL

I am convinced that bedtimes should be happy times and with my own children I would do anything to avoid them going to bed unhappy. I was always prepared to make concessions to them at this time. I would do my utmost to prevent any crying, and whereas during the day I might admonish or punish a small misdemeanour, it would go unmarked at night-time to make sure that my child didn't go to sleep with the sound of an angry parent's voice resounding in his ears.

If you have more than one child, let them enjoy their bedtimes in the same bedroom. Company is reassuring and seeing a sister or brother in pyjamas at the same time as her makes your child feel that bedtimes are just and fair, even if your older child is allowed to stay up slightly later. Until they get to an age where they need their privacy (see p. 30), it's a good idea for them to share a bedroom.

(see p. 30)

SLEEPING AWAY FROM HOME

It's quite reasonable for your child to be scared or refuse to get into a strange bed – for instance, when she goes to stay with friends or granny, or when you go on holiday.

* *Make the new bed into a playground: put lots of toys on the bed, and let your child have drinks and food on the bed so that she associates it with pleasant experiences.*

* *Show your child that you're in easy reach. Get her to call out and then answer her back so she knows you're close by.*

* *If she gets scared and refuses to use the bed, don't ridicule her, don't force her into bed, don't leave her alone, and don't lock the door of her bedroom; these tactics will only make her worse, so give it a break.*

* *Try telling her that because she is being so grown-up in using a new bed, she can have a treat, such as a new bedtime story or ten minutes' sitting on your knee watching television.*

FEAR OF THE DARK

As your child gets older and her imagination becomes more fertile, it's very easy for her to imagine frightening things in the shadows. A fear of the dark is entirely normal – even adults retain it. Leave a night-light on in the room or leave a light on outside with a dimmer switch so that your child can see her way to the bathroom if she needs it, or to your room if she's frightened. (If you use a night-light, make sure it doesn't cast frightening shadows.) Never insist on her bedroom being completely dark, and never ridicule her fear; it's really a sign that your child is growing up and learning about the world around her. Tell her that if she wakes up in the night and is frightened she can always come to you for a cuddle.

PRIVACY

You can encourage mature behaviour by providing your child with her own private space, which is hers alone, in which her belongings reside and where she can find her favourite things. Children respond very quickly to the idea of privacy, particularly if they are given a private space of their own that they can tidy up, be proud of and go to if they want to be quiet and play on their own.

You can teach your child to stay within her own space as early as two years, but certainly by three when she is open to reason. She'll learn that it's her responsibility not to disturb you thoughtlessly, just because she feels like it. Teaching her to respect your privacy is far better than shutting her out of your room, which you should never do.

You can affirm this sense of privacy by always pointing out to your child that certain things belong to her: this is her book, her toy, her dress, and they all have a proper place. In this way she will become familiar with her belongings and where she can find them. By about the age of four she's mature enough to realize that if she has her things, you have yours, too, and that just as she doesn't like her possessions being disturbed, neither do you.

DEVELOPMENT AND PLAY

Identifying and memorizing what's around him begins
the moment your child is born. As a parent, you can
help him to make sense of his surroundings.
During his first year, your baby's brain doubles in weight,
because thinking creates connections between brain
cells. "Learning to think" is a complex business of
building up associations culled from observing and
interacting with the world. Your child will not only
mature socially and mentally. He'll also become physically
skilled. He'll learn to sit, crawl and later to walk and
run, and he'll develop fine handling skills.

*Boys and girls have different
strengths and will develop
differently. In general, when
compared to boys, girls:*

• *Do better at language-based
skills, for instance talking,
reading and writing.*

• *Tend to be more sociable
and are more interested in
people than things.*

• *Usually walk earlier.*

• *Grow faster and are more
predictable and regular in
their growth patterns.*

• *Are better at jumping,
hopping and balance in the
preschool years.*

• *Are easier to get on with and
cope better with stress.*

Jumping
Contrary to expectations,
young girls are better than
boys at hopping and jumping.

YOUR DEVELOPING CHILD

There are a few general principles that apply to physical
development in all children. The stages or "milestones"
always follow the same order, since each one depends on
the previous stages. To give an obvious example, your child
cannot walk until he can stand.

Often a previously learned skill may appear to be
forgotten while your toddler is concentrating on learning a
new one, but will reappear when the new one is successfully
learnt. Sometimes a generalized activity makes way for a
specific one: at six months, your baby may make rather
random leg movements that resemble walking, but they are
quite different from the ones he will make when he actually
starts to walk at about one year.

One important physical milestone will be when your
baby's teeth start to come through. Although this might not
seem like a developmental step, teeth are essential to your
baby's learning to chew solid food and to speak properly.

MOVEMENT

All movement begins with the acquisition of head control.
Your child cannot sit up, stand up or crawl without being
able to control the position of his head. Development of
any kind proceeds from head to toe.

At first your baby's movements seem random, jerky and
quite unspecific (a newborn may move his arms, legs,
hands and feet when all he wants to do is smile). Gradually
over the next three years his movements are refined,
becoming increasingly specific to match the task in hand.

Crawling, though clever, is an inefficient and clumsy
way to get around, but your child has to learn balance and
co-ordination, and acquire self-confidence, before launching
himself into space.

Hearing and vision Your child's hearing is essential to his
development of speech, and there are various clues you can
look for very early on that indicate normal hearing: does he
turn towards the direction of a sound, or respond to your
voice by turning or smiling, for instance?

Your toddler's visual sense is now becoming highly
sophisticated. He already knows his colours and can
identify them. Although he may not be able to name
shapes, he can fit a diamond into a diamond shape, for
instance, and a square into a square shape. He can pick out

quite fine detail in a picture, and you can help this analytical phase of your toddler's visual development with suitable toys that you play with together.

Manipulation With the acquisition of a high degree of manual dexterity and five-finger movements, your toddler can start performing many delicate tasks – all seen as play to him, of course. He can turn a door-knob successfully, build simple toys that fit together and may even start to use children's scissors – a very complicated task for a toddler. He can also hold a pencil and a paintbrush in the adult way if he's been shown how to, and can draw and paint quite neatly if encouraged.

LEARNING TO THINK

Contact with new sights, sounds, smells, tastes and touches is what makes your toddler think, and that's why stimulation of all five senses is essential from birth. In order for your toddler to understand what's going on around him, he must use his senses, his intellect and his body to form mental connections so that he understands cause and effect. In order to pick up a favourite toy, for example, he must be able to see it, remember that he likes it, reach for it and then pick it up.

BECOMING SOCIABLE

Babies are born into the world able to both give and receive love from the outset, so we must both answer their demands for affection and respond to their need for it.

Babies become sociable by imitating us and will respond to a human voice from birth, so you should talk to your baby from the day he's born. Your child's personality and social skills can affect his achievement of developmental milestones. An independent and determined child will try new movements earlier than a more timid child, and a sociable child will seek social contact and communication with others and develop speech earlier than other children.

Your child's personality has three main components: sociability (the extent to which he seeks out and enjoys contact with other people), activity (his prowess at, and enjoyment of, movement and energy) and emotion (his tendency to mood swings). If any one of these traits is pronounced in your child, you should do your best to be accommodating, while at the same time encouraging the development of the other two qualities.

DEVELOPMENT IN BOYS

The pace of development, be it physical, intellectual or social, is affected by many things and gender is one of them; boys and girls develop according to different "time-tables". In general, when compared to girls, boys:

• *Begin to talk at a later stage and are more prone to language disorders.*

• *Tend to be less sociable and more interested in objects than in people.*

• *Usually walk later.*

• *Are more likely to grow in sudden spurts.*

• *Get better at jumping, running and throwing after the preschool years.*

• *Are more aggressive, competitive and rebellious.*

• *Are more vulnerable to stress and are more likely to have behavioural problems.*

Active play
Building toys encourage the development of your child's manipulative abilities.

Your child will grow and learn very rapidly in the first three years, so your choice of toys should reflect his changing needs.

- *Simple toys are more versatile so they have a longer life and are better for imaginative play.*

- *Toys with different colours, textures, shapes and noises will stimulate all five senses.*

- *Older babies enjoy games that involve building, particularly "put-in, take-out" toys, so bricks of different sizes are ideal.*

- *As your child's manipulative skills develop, he'll be able to manage interlocking blocks and more advanced shape-sorters.*

- *Preschool children enjoy drawing, painting and imaginative play, and simple games like snap or picture dominoes, which improve concentration.*

Painting
Give your child painting and drawing materials to allow him to develop his creativity.

HELPING YOUR CHILD

The first six weeks of life are a critical learning period for your baby in which you should be actively engaged. Your role as teacher starts at your baby's birth and continues for many years; it's your job to make his world an interesting and exciting place in which he can grow and learn.

From a very early age, your baby will recognize you, first by smell and sound, and enjoy a unique bond with you, which means that you are best equipped to teach him about his world, for even as adults we learn best from people with whom we feel comfortable or have a rapport. Your partner likewise has an important role to play. He should form a close and loving relationship with your baby as early as possible so that he becomes equally involved in teaching.

PROVIDING A GOOD ENVIRONMENT

To ensure a stimulating environment, surround your baby in the first six months with a wide variety of sounds, smells, sights and textures. In the early months your baby cannot interact with his surroundings in the way that he will once he learns to move and speak. His intellectual and emotional development, therefore, will be improved only through the different experiences you introduce to him.

When your child begins to play and walk, pay attention to the way he uses his toys. Make his playthings appealing by arranging them imaginatively and, rather than buying your child new toys all the time, encourage him to interact with existing toys in different ways – for example, by showing him how to use a cardboard box as a car or a boat. Often your child will get stimulation from improvised toys: a tent made out of a clothes rack and sheets, for instance, a balancing board, a little hill made out of turf, or a tunnel made from blankets and chairs, all provide the backdrop for imaginative play.

In practical terms, the area in which your child plays should be safe. Sandpits in the garden are ideal (but must be covered to prevent fouling by animals), or a corner of a room can be set aside specifically as a play area.

WORKING WITH YOUR CHILD

Responsible parents find that the role of teacher comes effortlessly and naturally. Your child is always eager to learn new things, so make the experience fun and mutually rewarding. Take any opportunity that presents itself – for example intimate moments of play or storytelling – to teach colours, textures, opposites and so on.

Teaching your child is not a formal process where specific rules and targets must be met. All teaching should be playful and be done with games. Feed your child's increasing curiosity and his need for new experiences. Introduce new concepts and answer his queries but, most importantly, praise him at every stage so that the learning process becomes unconscious and enjoyable, and one he wants to repeat over and over with you.

THE IMPORTANCE OF PLAY

Your child's development will centre around play and this is the most natural way for him to learn. It is only in the last twenty years that the full value of development through play has been recognized, since playing was previously regarded as an empty activity to fill the time when children could not be usefully employed. We now recognize that play is an essential means of acquiring the majority of adult skills, particularly social ones. Your child will first learn to form relationships and to share with children of his own age through play, and toys will have a significant educational role in all your child's developmental milestones.

Choose toys for their educational value. Reading, writing and counting proficiency require certain basic skills that your child will acquire through building and construction toys, playing with puzzles and jigsaws and matching colours, shapes and textures. The best toys are the ones that children return to again and again because they are limitless in their appeal – usually ones that encourage inventiveness. For this reason a household item like a whisk or sieve may give more lasting pleasure than many an expensive and elaborate toy. By sharing and encouraging your child in his play, you will strengthen the bond between you as he comes to see you as a giver of knowledge and fun.

Places to play It's nice to set aside a special activity space for your child – a sand tray, for example, or an area for messy play like painting or water games – but your child can play anywhere as long as you take the proper safety measures (see column, p. 36). The kitchen is an ideal place, provided you are there to keep an eye on your child. You could set up a dolls' corner where the dolls can be put to bed each evening and got up in the morning for breakfast.

TELEVISION

The average western child typically clocks up three hours' television viewing a day. One hour a day is plenty for your young child.

More than this may prevent your child from acquiring communication, imaginative and co-ordination skills that could be more thoroughly developed through games and storytelling. You should monitor the amount of television your child watches and be wary of using it as a convenient baby-sitting tool when you don't feel like amusing him. Used carefully, however, television can be a useful aid to acquiring new concepts, like telling the time.

Research shows that your child could continue to live in the fantasy world of television long after he's stopped watching, causing nightmares if he's watched anything frightening or violent.

Swedish researchers have shown that bringing your child back into the real world – with a story, tooth-brushing or laying out tomorrow's clothes – can banish this unpleasant effect of watching television.

SAFETY

As your baby's independence grows, a safe environment is increasingly important.

- *Stay close when your baby is taking his first steps and take particular care when he walks and creeps upstairs. Make sure the floor is not slippery and don't give him shoes until he's walking outdoors.*

- *Give your baby plenty of clear space for his walking attempts. Remove trailing flexes and small pieces of furniture.*

- *Fit safety gates to the top and bottom of your stairs. Gates at the top should open onto the landing and should not have horizontal bars that your baby could climb.*

- *Keep all poisonous substances well out of his reach and sight.*

Toys for walking
Your toddler's mobility and independence will be enhanced by sturdy, wheeled walking toys.

GETTING AROUND

Your baby will learn to walk on his own, but it's fun to help him practise if you have the time. Put your baby on his hands and knees and sit a short distance away. This will impel him to move towards you. He'll come more eagerly if you hold out your arms, call his name or offer a brightly coloured toy. To prompt your baby to twist, place a toy behind his back and support him as he turns around. When your baby reaches ten months he'll be able to stand up if supported by furniture. While he is standing and firmly supported, gently bend one of his knees and lift his foot; this will help him learn to step and bear his weight momentarily on one foot.

There's no right age for your baby to start to walk, but he's most likely to take his first unsupported steps between the ages of 9 and 15 months. When your baby is about 11 months, help him to practise walking forwards by holding his hands and guiding him. You can make cruising easier by positioning stable pieces of furniture close together around the room, but remove any items that could tip over easily when he pulls on them.

Improve your baby's stepping skills by calling to him while he is cruising around the room. Give him the courage to launch himself by moving the pieces of furniture further apart. Sit a little way from him and, while he is holding on to the furniture, hold out your arms and call him to you, but always be close enough to catch him if he stumbles.

At about 15 months, your baby can kneel, lower his body without support and stand up unaided. A chair with arms will allow your baby to sit down without falling and will provide good bending practice for his hips and knees.

Practise more leg movements with your baby, using a large soft ball that he can try to kick to you. This is also good for acquiring balance. Show him how to squat, and help him master hip and knee bends; they're all the more enjoyable if you do them to music. Games that use backwards or sideways steps will greatly increase his walking and balancing skills. "Ring-A-Rosy", a game in which you hold your baby's hands while walking, sitting and standing, is fun and lets him imitate you, making his achievement even greater.

MAKING PROGRESS

Between the ages of 18 months and three years your child will quickly progress in getting around. He will be very active on his feet, perfecting his walking and balancing skills, and you can encourage this development by involving him in your daily activities. He will begin to enjoy ball games, toys on wheels and games that involve hopping, jumping or climbing. Spend time with your child encouraging him in his new skills, building up his confidence and helping him to tackle new tasks that are difficult at first: it will be vital to his continuing physical development.

HOW TO HELP

Your child's toddler years are a time of great mental and physical activity for both of you. He will be interested in everything he sees and is developing the skills that will let him take part in a number of activities for the first time.

BALANCE IN GIRLS

Girls seem to be on a faster timetable than boys all the way through their growth; they tend to grow more regularly and predictably than boys.

In the preschool years girls are better at jumping, hopping and rhythmic movement and balance, so they will enjoy games that involve these. Hopscotch, skipping and dancing games will all give your little girl a chance to develop these skills.

21 months
Your child can now bend to pick up objects without falling over. He can walk with his arms by his sides and run quite well, but will find turning corners difficult and may topple over if he stops suddenly. He may be able to kick a ball, but rather awkwardly since he can't balance well on one leg.

Your child will automatically stretch out his arms to aid balance

2 years
Your child is more fluent at ball games, both catching and kicking, and can walk backwards as well as forwards. He can go up and down stairs without holding on, putting both his feet on each step. He can now veer and swerve while running and can stop running without falling over.

2½ years
Your child can now jump with both feet off the ground at the same time, walk on tiptoe and is steady on her feet. She can run quite well and glance over her shoulder without losing her balance.

BALANCE IN BOYS

In the preschool years there is little difference between boys and girls in terms of strength and speed.

Young boys achieve jumping, hopping, rhythmic movement and balancing skills less quickly than girls, so they tend to reach certain milestones later, such as picking up a toy from the floor without sitting down first. You should therefore give your little boy plenty of help with achieving these skills by allowing him freedom of movement. Games that involve kicking a ball, or dancing and jumping games, will all increase his skills.

Wheeled toys
A pushbike can be used indoors as well as out, and will improve your child's muscle strength and co-ordination.

This provides a great opportunity for you to involve him in many daily tasks which will be both fun for him and important to his development.

Give your child plenty of chances to practise his walking skills by going up and down stairs with him or leaving the pushchair behind on short trips. Hold his hand if he needs support or when you go out shopping. Alternatively, reins are even safer and will give your child more freedom, making them particularly suitable for use in the park or other playing areas. Don't put too many demands on his walking abilities at this stage – he won't be able to walk further than a few hundred metres. He is bound to have some lapses in his learning, so don't worry if he experiences setbacks in his walking like a stumble or fall – he will soon regain his confidence.

Agility in walking and running may also be developed by playing games that involve jumping and walking on tiptoe. Encourage your child to dance to music with you. He'll need plenty of practice at balancing, and this can be developed with ball games and other suitable toys. Start with a large, soft ball. Let him try walking along the top of a low wall, holding his hand all the time in case he gets a bit wobbly. Your child is probably too young for a bicycle, but a toy with wheels that he can sit on and propel with his feet will help develop his love of movement and strengthen his muscles. Indoors, give your child soft toys such as a mattress or foam rubber on which to jump and somersault. An outdoor swing will help develop strength and skills of co-ordination, but make sure both swing and garden are safe (see column, p. 40).

The more you involve your child in daily activities, such as cleaning, washing and climbing the stairs, the more teaching and practice he will receive. He will have enough co-ordination to help with tasks around the house, and he'll still see this as a form of play because he is so keen to imitate you. Take sensible precautions against falls and other household dangers, but don't worry unduly; toddlers are amazingly resilient and will be oblivious to most of the bruises they inevitably receive in these active and inquisitive years.

USING HIS HANDS

In terms of general development, the toddler stage marks a quite dramatic change from babyhood to childhood, and from the age of 18 months onwards you'll really notice this transformation, especially in manipulative skills. Over the next 18 months, your toddler will be getting more independent as he learns to dress himself and to manage increasingly fine movements. His creative skills also come to the fore at this stage as his building-block houses get more complicated and his drawings more recognizable.

ENCOURAGING SKILLS

All sorts of everyday tasks are now becoming possible for your child to manage by himself, so give him every opportunity to do things unaided. More complicated toys, especially construction or craft toys, will help him practise and develop his skills.

Dressing By the age of two, your child will be able to cope with a number of dressing skills, although putting on his socks, shoes and gloves will still be tricky, so let him choose his own clothes and practise getting dressed. Clothes with press studs and fairly large buttons, provided the holes are not too tight, will also encourage him to develop new

ENCOURAGING INDEPENDENCE

With so many new skills to learn at this stage, it is important not to expect your child to develop at a rate that is too fast for him.

All children progress at their own pace, which is decided by the speed that their developing brain and nerves allow. Your child will want to please you, and may try to do things.that are more complicated than his development will allow.

Failure is demoralizing because he feels he's let you down. A better approach is to give him all the help and encouragement he needs, showing him how pleased you are with every task he manages, without setting him unrealistic goals that are beyond his abilities.

Joining the blocks is an intricate task

Doing up buttons develops finger skills

Learning to dress
Encourage your child's interest in dressing himself by letting him choose the clothes he is to wear.

Construction toys
Interlocking building blocks are always popular toys and are ideal for developing hand movements.

OUTDOOR SAFETY

Your child will love to explore a different environment, but make sure that you follow some basic safety guidelines.

• *Keep garden gates locked with child-resistant locks.*

• *Install swings, slides and climbing toys on grass or sand, never concrete or paving. Check regularly for strength, stability and signs of corrosion.*

• *Check all play equipment to ensure that there is no risk of scissoring, shearing or pinching injuries and that surfaces are free from snags and splinters.*

• *Instruct children carefully on what they can and can't do on play equipment.*

Crafts
Your three- or three-and-a-half-year-old's ability to use scissors is a huge step forward in manual dexterity and brain–muscle co-ordination. Give him simple models to make. Any scissors he uses should be blunt-ended.

finger skills. Continue to encourage his dressing ability and he will soon be able to put on and take off underpants, trousers and T-shirts. Once he can manage all his buttons, including the smaller ones, he will be able to dress and undress himself completely, as long as the fastenings are all easy for him to reach.

Improving dexterity As soon as your child can turn a door knob with two hands and open a loose-fitting screw-top jar, give him toys that need to be fitted together. Washing and drying his hands will also be a favourite pastime so encourage him in this. Ensure that your two-year-old has plenty of colourful picture books to hand as he can now turn the pages of a book one at a time by himself. Your child can now build a tower of four blocks and with encouragement he'll make more complicated structures. Building blocks that need pressing and fitting together will help develop the small movements of his hands. Intricate tasks such as threading large beads on to a piece of string or fitting together jigsaw puzzles made of large pieces will boost his manipulation skills.

Arts and crafts Children enjoy drawing at this age, so give your child plenty of drawing materials, including a range of different crayons, and start him off by showing the effects of all the different colours. He will also enjoy using paints, especially if you allow him to be messy and paint with his hands. You can also help him relate his drawings to the world around him by naming the colours of the crayons and then pointing out the same colours in everyday objects. He will soon be producing images of people and objects that are familiar to him, and by two-and-a-half years his pictures will become more recognizable.

At three years old, your child is maturing rapidly. He can draw and colour quite accurately and his drawings are becoming more recognizable and accomplished as he begins to master skills like copying two straight lines drawn at right angles. By the age of four he will have mastered the complicated action of using scissors. Building blocks are becoming too simple for him, so he is ready to move on to more sophisticated construction sets. He is already doing very simple tasks around the house, and from four years old he will get much better at jobs such as setting the table, washing his face and hands, making his bed, and putting his clothes tidily away at the end of the day.

MENTAL DEVELOPMENT

Your baby is born with a finite number of brain cells, yet his brain doubles in weight between birth and 12 months. The increase in weight is due to the growth of connections between the different cells used in thinking. When your baby sees a piece of bread, points to it, reaches for it, picks it up, puts it in his mouth, chews it, tastes it and swallows it, he's built up eight brain connections and slotted it all into his memory.

THE PARENT'S ROLE

Very few children are retarded, and equally few are especially gifted, so the chances are that your child falls within the normal range of intelligence. Your task as a parent is to accept his abilities and to help him develop his strengths by careful teaching. Remember, too, that there are many fields of ability: we tend to think of intelligence rather narrowly as verbal and arithmetic skills, but your child may have creative and artistic abilities that are just as valuable and just as much in need of nurturing. Never push your child: accept him for who he is, give him every opportunity to develop his talents; show him and let him know that you love and respect him just as he is.

INTELLIGENCE TESTING

Modern systems of intelligence testing were developed in 1905 by two Frenchmen. Originally they were intended to predict whether children were likely to do well at school, and concentrated on judgement, comprehension and reasoning (continued p. 42). (continued p. 42)

Making costumes
Encourage your child to make his own dressing-up toys with a variety of coloured card, crayons, scissors and sticky tape.

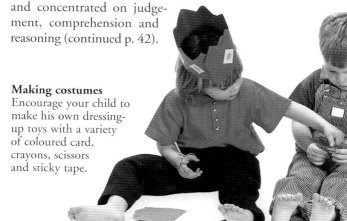

THE FEMALE BRAIN

When a baby girl is born, her brain is already sexed, that is, programmed for femaleness. Brain structure is responsible for many developmental differences between boys and girls.

- *In the womb, the cortex, which determines intellect, develops sooner in girls than in boys.*

- *The left half of the cortex, which controls thinking, develops earlier in girls than in boys.*

- *The earlier development of the left side of the brain in girls confers greater language-related skills on girls than boys.*

- *The corpus callosum, the part of the brain that connects the right lobe to the left, is better developed in girls.*

- *The two sides of the brain "talk" to each other earlier and better in girls; this gives them an advantage in reading, a skill that uses both sides of the brain.*

- *Girls show earlier and greater fear on separation than boys because their nervous connections mature earlier. This leads to faster message transmission than in boys and so girls recognize earlier what's going on around them.*

THE MALE BRAIN

Even while your baby is in the womb, his brain is programmed for maleness. Differences in brain structure and function between boys and girls affect the way they develop as they grow up.

• *A boy's brain weight and volume are greater than a girl's by about 10–15 percent.*

• *When the right side of the brain is ready to send connections to the left, the appropriate cells don't yet exist in boys. As a result the fibres go back into the right side. This enriches connections within the right lobe and could explain why boys have greater spatial awareness than girls.*

• *Boys show less fear on separation than girls because they have slower message transmission until the brain matures. Also, from as early as nine or ten months, they bring the fear of separation under control by activity such as playing with a toy or crawling to investigate an object so as to distract themselves. This mode of behaviour continues right into adulthood.*

Modern testing views intelligence as the ability to process information, and so the tests are devised to see how well a child is acquiring thinking skills and applying them to everyday life. They are limited to skills that are important at school, and don't take account of creativity or artistic talent. It is wrong to use IQ scores to predict how successful a child will be in later life, since thinking skills develop over time.

CREATIVITY

All children have some creative ability, and developing this in the preschool years is just as important as teaching letters and numbers. There are a whole range of skills and mental processes that you can encourage in your child to stimulate his creative abilities: point out the things happening around him, show him patterns, colours, flowers, animals and smells, act out empathy for other people, talk about feelings, invent stories and imagine "What would happen if…?". Dressing up, painting and drawing, or making toys are all practical activities that can help your child develop his creativity and imagination.

MILESTONES

18 months He'll ask for food, drinks and toys. He's on the verge of his first step towards bladder control when he grunts to attract your attention and points to his nappy as he passes urine. He will carry out several simple requests and begin to understand more complex ones, such as "Please get your hairbrush from the bathroom". He may also grab your arm or use other gestures to get your attention. His vocabulary may consist of about 30 words.

2 years Your child's vocabulary of names and objects will increase rapidly. He will describe and identify familiar items. He will obey complicated orders, and find a toy that he played with before. He will talk non-stop and ask occasional questions.

Shortly after this he will know who he is and say his own name. He'll try to build houses and castles with blocks, and repeat new words when encouraged. He'll begin to pit his will against yours and may become rather negative – saying "no" fairly often and not always fitting in with your wishes. He may know the difference between one and several, but he has little idea of the magnitude of numbers and so anything more than one may be "lots".

2½–3 years Your child will start to add detail to broad concepts, as in "A horse has a long tail", and be able to draw horizontal and vertical lines. He'll be able to say one or two nursery rhymes and find them in his book, and he'll know some colours. He will also ask "why?" and say "won't" and "can't". He may make an attempt at copying a circle that you have drawn for him (see right), but probably won't be able to complete it. Your child will now enjoy helping with household tasks. He will begin to grasp the concept of numbers and may be able to count to three. A boy will have noticed that his sex organs stick out from his body, in contrast to those of little girls he has seen.

Your child can understand prepositions, such as "in", "on", "under", "behind" and "after". At around three years old, he'll be able to form more complex sentences and his vocabulary may consist of 200–300 words. This, together with his ever-increasing curiosity, will lead him to ask incessant questions. He can distinguish between "now" and "then" and will refer to the past. He knows his own gender. He'll become more sociable and like to play with others.

DRAWING

Your child's improving manual dexterity is clearly demonstrated by his ability to copy a circle.

- *At two-and-a-half years, his attempts at a circle may end up as a continuous round shape, like a spiral.*

- *At three years, his attempts become more controlled, but the circle may not quite join up or the lines may overshoot.*

- *At three-and-a-half years, your child should be able to draw a closed figure, either a true circle or an oval shape.*

REASONING

Your child is starting to think about and learn from his experiences. Information is sifted, matched up to other experiences to see if they fit together, or if they differ greatly, and it is then put into similar or different pigeonholes. Your child is learning to reason.

Your child starts to plan ahead, and becomes much more creative and imaginative. Gradually all the information that he has absorbed so far becomes available to apply to a given situation. This new ability to think, imagine and create, changes your child's perception of the world considerably.

Many familiar things in the house or garden no longer contain the same interest. He needs wider horizons; he needs to explore, to push the frontiers of his experience and knowledge further and further forwards. Your child becomes very interested in how things work. He is greedy for information and is constantly asking "why?".

A huge step is realizing that time is not just in the present: there is today, yesterday and tomorrow. Planning for the future is one of the most critical

Chores
Your toddler enjoys helping you with some simple household tasks, such as sweeping.

COLOURS

To help your child grasp the notion of colour, mention the colour of something that you are using or wanting.

- *Household items: "I'm looking for the green packet"; "Where's that red tin gone?"; "Oh, I've found the jar with the blue label".*

- *Your child's clothes: "That's a pretty pink dress"; "What a nice red jumper".*

- *Flowers, animals and especially birds: "Can you see the robin's red breast?".*

- *Show your child how colours are made: "Look, if we mix a little bit of red with this white we'll get pink; yellow mixed with blue will make green".*

- *Teach your child the seven colours of the rainbow and get him to pick them out if you see a real rainbow.*

Concept of roundness
A toddler can begin to deal with quite sophisticated ideas. He'll understand, for example, that roundness is a property of different objects.

aspects of our intellect and it is during this third year that you will hear your child say for the first time, "I will eat that later", or "We can go tomorrow".

FORMING CONCEPTS

This is an important step forward for your child. One way in which it will be obvious is when, between the ages of 18 months and two years, he starts sorting objects as a form of play: he might sort his building blocks out from his other toys, for example, or the different animals in a toy farmyard. You'll notice, too, that he's begun to understand how things are grouped: he knows, for instance, that his toy ball and an apple are similar in shape and that they roll; that sparrows and crows are alike because they have feathers and fly; that animals that bark and have four legs are dogs.

Some time before his third birthday, your toddler will begin to give these concepts names – round, bird, dog. He will use the names where they are appropriate – whether the dog in question, for instance, is a family pet, a dog he sees in a book, or a toy dog. By the time your toddler is three years old he will describe things in a way that shows he also understands their differences: "our dog", "toy dog".

LEARNING THROUGH PLAY

Play helps learning in many ways. It improves manual dexterity – building a tower of blocks or doing a jigsaw puzzle teaches a child how to make his hands work for him as tools. Playing with other children teaches him it's important to get on with other people; he'll discover friendship and learn to be kind and considerate to others.

Social play helps to make a child's language more sophisticated because the more imaginative the play, the more complex the ideas that have to be put into words. Play aids physical development; the freedom to swing, climb, skip, run and jump helps to perfect muscular co-ordination and physical skills. Play also improves hearing and vision considerably.

TYPES OF PLAY

Girls and boys love dolls; dolls are children's pretend families, helping them to create a make-believe world into which children can escape. While playing with dolls, your child is learning to understand human emotions. A girl will mother the doll, give it instructions, then dress it, put it to bed and kiss it goodnight. In this way she is re-enacting the things that happen to her, and learning to relate them to other people. Even action dolls for boys can bring out protective feelings. A child can also use dolls to get rid of aggressive instincts that might otherwise be directed against other children.

An important concept for a child to grasp is whether things are the same or different. Toys of farmyard animals can help form this idea; if your child plays with toy sheep, horses and chickens, he'll be able to sort out the animals that look the same. You can help by showing him the differences and naming the animals as you put them into groups.

Children love playing with water, especially in the bath. Give your child empty plastic bottles and containers so he can create a variety of water effects. All children love blowing bubbles; put some washing-up liquid in a beaker, and give him a pipe-cleaner with a circle shaped at one end. Paddling pools, like the small blow-up kind, are ideal in the summer and needn't be expensive. Another summer game is to lay a tarpaulin on the ground and spray a hose over it; your child will enjoy sliding around on the slippery surface.

Painting encourages your child's creative urges. He'll love finger-painting and will be able to produce a range of interesting prints and patterns with combs, pegs, sponges, cotton reels or cardboard tubes. Try cutting star shapes and other simple patterns out of pieces of potato so he can create unusual designs of his own. Plastic egg boxes or baking trays will make good palettes for the aspiring painter. Give your child big brushes with thick bristles so that he sees bold results immediately. Provide pastry brushes, large cotton wool balls, corks, plastic straws and pipe-cleaners for variety and extra stimulation.

Costumes
Children love dressing up, so stock a box with old shoes, shirts, skirts, dresses, trousers, jackets, hats and scarves to fuel their imagination, and include some cheap jewellery.

IMAGINATION

Most children over the age of 15 months or so begin to develop a vivid imagination, and there are substantial individual differences. In general, the greater the intelligence of a child the greater the imagination.

Between 15 and 18 months, imagination begins to appear in doll play. At three years, your child will have imaginary playmates behind the sofa and he will tell tall stories and play highly imaginative games with friends. His imagination may lead to the development of fears: of the dark, of noises or of animals, for example.

LANGUAGE IN GIRLS

Right from the moment of birth, girls are more responsive to the human voice than boys, and they have better verbal skills throughout childhood.

Girls talk earlier than boys, and begin to string words into sentences earlier. They have better articulation, pronunciation and grammar, and are better at verbal reasoning. They also learn to read earlier than boys.

The structure of the female brain is believed to be the reason for girls' superior verbal skills (see column, p. 41): the speech centres are more tightly organized in the female brain than in the male brain, and have more and better connections with other functions of the brain.

LEARNING TO TALK

Your toddler is learning new words all the time now and he's also starting to put them together. His pronunciation will be indistinct, but this is no cause for worry; if he is using words with meaning and putting them together, then his language is developing. Mild speech defects, such as lisping, are very common in children, and usually disappear without any treatment. There is great variation in the speed at which children acquire speech, so don't feel the need to compare your child with others of his age, and don't worry if his development doesn't match the timetable given here: I give these dates merely as average guidelines, and no child corresponds exactly to the average.

HOW VOCABULARY INCREASES

18 months – 2 years Your child's speech will become more complex during this time. He'll probably have a vocabulary of about 30 words, including possessives ("mine"), and negatives ("won't"), instead of simply "no". He's starting to combine words to make simple statements, such as "ball gone", or questions: "Where Daddy?" He understands that conversation is a two-way thing and will wait his turn to speak, and he uses language to give information, to ask for things, to tell how he feels, or to relate to other people.

Remember that he can understand a lot more words than he can use, so you can continue to help him by teaching him new words. Use adjectives whenever you can, and combine them with nouns: "good boy", "hot water", "big dog". Introduce adverbs too: "Run quickly", "Pat the dog gently". When you use prepositions, such as "on", "under", "behind", always show him what you mean.

2–3 years By now your toddler probably has a vocabulary of 200–300 words, and he can talk at some length. He's interested in learning new words, his attention span is longer, and he will listen to you when you explain things or give reasons. He will still mispronounce words, and may lisp, but his fluency and confidence are improving all the time. He can connect two ideas in a single sentence – "I get teddy and play in garden" – and can use pronouns such as "I", "me" and "you" correctly.

You can help your child to increase his vocabulary by using unfamiliar words in your speech in such a way that he can guess at their meaning, and repeat them frequently so that he can learn how they are used. Encouraging an interest in books is probably the best single thing you can do for your child, so read to him often, and explain new words as they arise. He will like to hear the same stories read over and over again, and will be able to understand increasingly complicated narratives.

Your child's use of language is becoming more social now, and he will talk more to other children than to adults, so contact with children is the best way to help him develop his abilities.

3 years Your child will enjoy learning new words, so he listens to adult conversations carefully, and his attention span is increasing. He can understand words that describe how he feels, such as "cold", "tired", "hungry". He is also beginning to understand words such as "on", "under" and "behind", although this will take longer. He should be able to give his first and last name. His mind is racing ahead of his ability to form words at this stage, so he may start to stutter, but this is likely to be temporary. If he hasn't overcome his stutter by about four-and-a-half, or earlier if it is severe, it might be worth consulting a speech therapist.

4 years Children of this age talk a great deal: they boast, exaggerate, tell tall tales and have conversations with imaginary friends. Your child will ask lots of questions, as much out of a desire to keep you talking as out of any real curiosity, because he loves conversation. He will enjoy inventing silly words, and may indulge in mildly obscene verbal play, especially to do with the lavatory and the potty. He will probably start to use slang, and he may call you names and threaten you.

LANGUAGE IN BOYS

Boys are almost always slower than girls at developing language skills, and this discrepancy lasts right through childhood.

Boys are later in talking than girls, are slower to put words together in sentences and take longer to learn to read. Speech disorders such as stuttering are far more common in boys than in girls, and boys outnumber girls in remedial reading classes by four to one.

Although this difference in linguistic ability levels out somewhat during the teenage years, you can help your son's language skills in the preschool years by reading aloud to him and playing lots of word games.

Socializing
During the third year, your child's verbal skills will be improved by talking to other children.

WHAT YOU CAN DO TO HELP

There are many ways you can help your child as he becomes more skilled and confident in using language.

• *Never overtly correct your child's mistakes; diplomatically repeat what he has just said, but correctly. If he hesitates over a word, supply it instantly to maintain his momentum.*

• *Your child responds well to reasoning, so include him in simple problem solving, with questions, options and solutions, openly discussing each step. Ask his opinion about something you know you can agree with so that he feels he is included and has made the decisions.*

• *When your child speaks to you, turn to him and listen attentively. Nod, and incline your head to show you are listening to him.*

• *In your child's list of reading, include a choice of fairy stories, because they help your child to come to terms with his own world without it hurting him, and because they improve his concepts of real and unreal; past, present and future; fairness and injustice; good and evil, and so on.*

5 years Your five-year-old will ask innumerable questions, and now he really is seeking new information. He loves to be read to. He is aware that there is a "right" way to say things and will often ask you what it is. He can understand opposites, and it's very easy to make a game out of this, where you give a word such as "soft", "up", "cold" and he has to give the opposite. He will also be able to define words if you ask him, and this is a very good way of getting him to use his skills of classification as well as verbal skills. In fact all word games are excellent mental exercise, because clear speaking goes hand in hand with clear thinking.

LANGUAGE AND UNDERSTANDING

You will be able to observe the way your child gradually gains concepts in his use of language. He will often use the same word to describe similar things, so that apples, oranges and peaches are all "apple", because they are all round and fruit; and horses, cows and sheep are all "horse" because they are all large animals with four legs. This doesn't necessarily mean that he can't tell the difference, only that he doesn't have words to describe all of them, so he uses the nearest one.

Similarly, the questions your child asks you may be very simple because he can't fully express what it is he wants to know. So when he says "What's that", he may be asking "What is it? What is it called? What does it do? How does it work?" all at once. Give him as much information as you think he can understand: "This is washing powder. It's just like soap, and I put it in the washing machine to make our clothes lovely and clean." Always try to answer the question he is really asking.

Girls at play
Close friendships form the basis of a girl's social world, and this will be reflected in her choice of language.

BECOMING SOCIABLE

Your newborn baby needs to interact socially, especially with you, his parents. He learns to be sociable by imitating you, first with facial expressions, then with gestures and movements and finally with complete patterns of behaviour. In this way the relationship between parent and child forms the blueprint for all subsequent relationships, so it is your responsibility to be more aware of your behaviour and responses than ever before. From the moment you start to talk to your baby he begins to develop into a social being because he longs to communicate and converse with you.

Like all other development, social development has its own well-defined stages. Everyone has heard of the "Terrible Twos" when your child enters a stage of refusing to obey, and of doing what he is told not to do. This is his way of asserting his independence and, although at times you'll believe that it will go on forever, it's simply a stage in his learning to interact with other people.

DEVELOPING PERSONALITY

It would be marvellous if we could predict the future personality of a child when he was still an infant. Certainly we can do so with intelligence. Personality and character, however, derive partly from heredity and partly from environment so there always remains the possibility that, as the result of a bad environment or the lack of secure, loving relationships, a child may not have the opportunities to grow up as a loving and lovable adult.

In view of the profound effect of environment and family on character, predictions during a child's infancy are doomed to failure. However, observant parents can detect differences in their children's personalities from the outset. Perhaps it's a good thing that predicting how a child's personality will develop is so difficult. From the point of view of adoption it would be a pity if such predictions were possible. Adoptive parents have a right to want to know the intelligence of the child whom they are thinking of adopting. They must not expect to know what his personality will be like. All parents take huge risks when having children, not even knowing if they will be mentally normal. If they're not willing to take that risk they should not consider having children.

GIRLS'
BEHAVIOUR

Girls tend to develop social skills and enjoy the company of other people far earlier than boys do. While no child conforms to a stereotype, in general, girls:

- *Are more sociable than boys, and form closer friendships from an earlier age.*

- *Are more compliant with adult requests than boys tend to be in early childhood.*

- *Show fewer competitive traits and are less socially aggressive and dominant than boys.*

- *Cope far more easily with physical, emotional and intellectual stress than boys.*

BOYS' BEHAVIOUR

Boys tend to be slower to develop social skills than girls, but not all boys will show the following traits to a marked degree. The point of knowing these difficulties with social development is so that you can always be on the lookout to help, encourage and praise your child's efforts. Broadly speaking, boys:

• Tend to be slower to develop social skills than girls.

• Are far more socially aggressive than girls.

• Have more friendships than girls, but they tend to be superficial and short-lived.

• Are more emotionally vulnerable than girls.

• Tend to have more behavioural problems, particularly when around authority figures.

INDIVIDUALITY

Your baby's individuality will gradually become more and more apparent as he grows and learns. You should treasure your baby's individuality and nurture his growth and strength. The gradual insight you gain into your baby's personality is like watching a thrilling film in slow motion. All his preferences, the things that make him laugh and cry, the foods he likes, his favourite toys, come together to create his unique personality.

BEGINNING TO SOCIALIZE

From his first moments your baby looked to you as the centre of his world – the main provider of affection and care. However, as he gets older and his self-awareness and life experiences develop, he'll begin to see you as a separate person and will extend his interest to other people. Although you cannot make friends for him, you can help by introducing him to a few first companions. He will soon learn to adapt his skills and develop the social habits of older boys and girls.

18 months – 2 years At this age you should encourage your child to interact with other children. Invite children to the house and give him games and play material to facilitate socializing. Be patient; although his first reaction may be self-centred, he will modify selfish behaviour if it is played down and his achievements are praised.

2–2½ years As he is learning to share, encourage games that involve giving to others and respecting their wishes. He may demonstrate feelings of rivalry as a consequence and try to force his will on others. You will need to use discipline fairly while still encouraging and supporting all his efforts and achievements, since approval is more important at this stage.

2½–3 years As your child continues to socialize, he becomes increasingly independent from you and more outgoing towards other children.

Social skills
Toddlers play alongside each other rather than together, but will enjoy the company.

He will start to be more generous and unselfish in play with others, and form stronger friendships with adults and children, showing signs of sympathy when others are in distress. Always encourage your child to be truthful and honest in relationships with others.

RIGHT AND WRONG

Your child will learn the differences between right and wrong only if they are clearly pointed out. In the first year you can use sounds and actions to act out why hot or sharp things are dangerous. If your child understands why you want him to do something he is much more likely to do it willingly, so try to explain and then ask his opinion. There are situations that are non-negotiable: when your child's safety is threatened, when the thoughts and feelings of others should be considered, and when your child is tempted to tamper with the truth. You should be very firm on these points, and he will gradually learn a sense of responsibility for disciplining himself as he grows up. Cheekiness can often be mistaken for impertinence, but unless your child is imposing on the feelings of others, he may be displaying nothing more than a healthy resistance to authority which can be useful, if sensibly directed.

A spoilt or over-indulged child will behave in a self-centred way and this may be the result of his parents being over-protective, displaying favouritism or having high expectations for him. The best cure is to let him go to playgroup or preschool at two-and-a-half to three in order to get him used to mixing with other children.

SHARING

Young children are naturally selfish and usually begin to think of others only when they're taught to do so. Your child has to understand that other children feel as he does before he is able to grasp the importance of thinking of other people's feelings. Do not worry if your child seems to be slow in learning to share; it's very difficult, but with your patience he will successfully acquire this skill.

DEVELOPING FRIENDSHIPS

Just like all the other lessons he has to learn through life, your child's ability to make friends could be slow to develop, so introduce it to him gradually. Invite friends around, one at a time to begin with, to a familiar home

IDENTIFYING WITH OTHERS

By the time your child reaches the age of three he will begin the process of identification, both with himself and with other people around him.

You will start to see evidence of his self-awareness as he takes steps to command and control himself, showing that he can put himself in the position of others. You may overhear your child scolding himself when he thinks he has done something that you would disapprove of. He will begin to act out the part of the adults who are known to him, particularly you, frequently adopting phrases that you use regularly.

This will all become part of the process of him exploring and getting to know the way the world works and his own part in it. Now is the time to introduce him to the idea of a wider circle of people, teaching him to respect and be polite to them. Introduce him to visitors to the house – delivery people, the postman and window cleaner – as well as your own friends, and make meeting people part of his daily routine.

GROWING UP LIKE MUM

By the age of three your little girl is aware of the fact that she is female and that she'll grow up to be a woman.

This makes her very attentive to you – her mother. Her view of gender roles will be influenced by your attitudes. If you:

• Regard yourself as equal to your partner, your daughter will see this as normal.

• Treat other women as close friends and confidantes, your daughter will see relationships with adult women in this way.

• See working as integral to family life, your daughter will view a career as compatible with having a family.

environment where he is sure of himself. Be near at hand to give him help and support should he need it. He will then begin to build up a small circle of friends and gain confidence through his own place in it – an essential way to learn the ground rules for future friendships.

Shyness is something that affects many children. Common types of shy behaviour include disliking new experiences, social gatherings, talking to unknown people and having difficulty in making friends. Don't think of shyness as something wrong with your child; many well-adjusted adults are quite shy. The best way of dealing with it is not by criticism or forcing change, but by preparing your child for any situation he's likely to find difficult.

Excessive shyness does not mean that your child is retarded, and you should avoid becoming over-protective and over-anxious. In most cases time and patience are all that is needed to help him gain a sense of security.

INCREASING INDEPENDENCE

Your preschooler faces many changes in how he sees himself as his independence grows and his personality matures. Sudden upheavals can cause your child to exhibit quite violent changes of mood as he tries to relate his changing identity to his family life and the guidelines he has learnt for social behaviour, both of which are relatively constant. Be patient and allow him to mature in his own time. The difficult stages are easily outweighed by the thrilling ones, and your child must experience both in order to become a socially adept member of his community.

If your child has been brought up to relate to new friends he will separate from you easily from the age of three-and-a-half onwards, and at about the same time he will learn to play interactive games such as tag. He will be generous and generally sympathetic when someone else is distressed.

A SENSE OF IDENTITY

By the time he is three years old, your child already has an interest in his own gender and in the way he is different from the opposite sex. At about the age of three-and-a-half he'll express "I like" and then slightly later "I love" and he will affirm, if questioned, that he is a boy rather than a girl. He will begin to express interest in physiological differences between the genders and in boys' and girls' postures for urinating. He makes no distinctions between gender at play and realizes that people touch out of friendship as well as out of love. He begins to become interested in babies and wants his family to have one. He will ask questions such as "What can the baby do when it comes?" or "Where does it come from?". Although most three-year-olds don't understand all the answers (for example, that the baby grows inside its mother), it is still vital that you answer your child's questions as frankly and honestly as possible so that his trust in you is not undermined.

RELATIONSHIPS

Children who grow up in a stable, secure environment and feel loved by their parents are likely to become well-adjusted adults. Ideally, you and your partner will have equal but complementary roles: you have authority over some situations, your partner has authority over others, so that your child cannot play one of you against the other. The way a child interacts with his parents and siblings evolves gradually between the ages of three and five.

MOTHER AND CHILD

At the age of three, children usually have good relationships with their mothers. Quite often the mother is the favourite parent with whom children like to discuss and relive past events. By three-and-a-half the mother–child relationship can sometimes become more difficult. Children can be simultaneously demanding and resistant. A child may refuse to eat, dress or take a nap for his mother, but be quite compliant with someone else.

By the age of four your child will take pride in you, quote things that you say and boast about you to friends, although at home he'll still resist your authority.

FATHER AND CHILD

At three years the mother tends to be the favourite parent, but the father can take over in many situations. For instance, a child may cling less at bedtime and go to sleep more quickly in the presence of the father. At the age of three-and-a-half, girls may express closeness to their fathers.

At four, children boast about their fathers outside the home, and quote them as an authority. Some children may feel jealous of their father spending a lot of time with their mother and feel they're being deprived of her attention. A child may then verbally express dislike for his father.

GROWING UP LIKE DAD

Your little boy will have realized by the age of three that he will grow up to be a man, and he will become particularly interested in his father.

Your little boy will watch your partner and learn from him what it is to be a man. If your partner:

- *Treats women, particularly you or his daughters, in a caring and considerate way, your little boy will believe that this is the correct way to treat women.*

- *Sees other men as friends, your son will also find older men approachable.*

- *Enjoys and participates in family life, your child will follow this example.*

- *Resolves disputes with rudeness and violence, your child will do so too.*

TWINS

*The extra-strong bond that
exists between twins is
legendary; they have a close
and intuitive understanding
of each other. But from the
outset it's only fair to twins to
think of them and treat them
as individuals.*

*Choosing names that sound
very different and dressing
twins differently will encourage
their individual sense of
identity. Different coloured
bed-linen and towels help too.*

*Nearly half of all twins develop
a secret language so weird it
excludes the adult world.
Milestones can be late, not just
with speech but with handling
skills too. Twins share the
parental attention that a single
child would enjoy undiluted
and so there are fewer chances
to learn. Try to talk as freely to
the quiet twin as to the
questioning one.*

*Make sure your twins feel at
home with any social group, be
it family or friends, or toddlers,
from a very early age. There's a
danger of not mixing with
other children because twins
have each other for company.*

*In a new group, others may
find twins rather bossy and
self-centred. Twins may also
opt to remain a twosome apart
from other children, and will
have to be persuaded to join
in. Gradual separation can
often work if activities are split
between parents and friends.
Dad might get one twin to
help in the garden while Mum
takes the other shopping.*

SIBLINGS

At the age of four, relationships with siblings can be turbulent. A child is old enough to be a nuisance to older siblings and can be selfish, rough and impatient with younger siblings. Quarrels and physical fights over toys and possessions are common and there will be complaints about fairness: "He's got more than me!".

A five-year-old child is usually good with younger brothers and sisters. Girls, particularly, can be protective and kind towards younger members of the family, and are helpful rather than domineering. Having said this, a five-year-old is still too young to be responsible for looking after younger siblings; and although he may be caring while an adult is present, your child may resort to teasing when left alone with a younger sister or brother. Five-year-olds usually interact well with older siblings, sometimes adopting the role of baby in domestic play.

THE ONLY CHILD

Although there are benefits to being an only child, such as having lots of love and attention, there are also disadvantages. Without the presence of other children of a comparable age, the only child can sometimes feel lonely, and reticent about mixing in groups. As long as you are aware of this, you can do things to compensate. It is important to introduce your child to other children at an early age. Encourage him to invite friends home and to visit other friends' houses, and arrange outings with other young children.

Another problem associated with only children is the tendency that some parents have to be possessive and over-protective. This can be dangerous for both parent and child. Your child may become timid and wary of new people and experiences if you don't allow him a sense of adventure and the freedom to experiment and explore. Parents, meanwhile, will have a more acute sense of loss when the child does become independent.

An only child needs the same amount of discipline as other children. Try not to be over-indulgent, and make your child realize that he cannot always expect to have your undivided attention.

FAMILY LIFE

Having a toddler in the family sometimes seems like living with an unguided missile: toddlers are adventurous, curious, into everything the moment you turn your back and they often leave a trail of mayhem behind them. Toddlers have not yet acquired the judgment to match their strength of will and clashes with you will probably be frequent, possibly ending up with temper tantrums. Never fear – it's all worth it. Most of the time they let their charm, intelligence, wit and affability shine through and you'll find it's a time you remember with fondness and nostalgia when they're older.

Learning to look after your new baby in the first weeks can be overwhelming, so look after yourself, too.

- *Get your partner to help out with the baby so you can have some time to yourself.*

- *Don't expect to be a perfect mother straight away. You have a lot to learn, and your baby is learning too.*

- *Let the housework go. Do only the essential tasks, and get someone else to do them if you can.*

- *Low potassium levels can contribute to a feeling of exhaustion. Eat plenty of potassium-rich foods, such as bananas, tomatoes, dried apricots and plain yogurt.*

ORGANIZING YOUR LIFE

As any mother knows, the physical, emotional and social demands on your life seem to multiply unendingly with the increased mobility of your toddler. Hectic, demanding and tiring days, coupled with the psychological pressure of having to guide and teach your emerging preschooler, combine to heap unexpected stress on you as a family.

Organization can be the key to survival. If things seem to be getting on top of you, sit down and take stock of the situation before you are swept away by the joys and traumas of toddlerhood. No matter what stage you are at, it is never too late to organize your time so that you get more out of it.

When you are planning your family life, try dividing up things you have to think about into three or four areas: toddler-related, work-related (house and/or office), partner-related and you. This fourth category happens to be one of the most important, but is usually undervalued. If you aren't happy, your toddler won't be happy. There are certain things that you will find helpful to think about in advance. For instance, if you are a working mother, have you spoken to your manager about the possibility of working flexi-time? Have you considered going back but doing reduced hours? Is it possible for you to do a job-share?

If you will be working part-time, will any of your working rights be affected? They shouldn't be, but you should check now rather than finding out later on. You don't want to discover that you might be facing a wage cut when you've already committed yourself to expensive child care.

TIME FOR YOURSELF

You are your child's universe, so it's best for her if you're not irritable, grumpy and feeling jaded. While you must make every effort to meet your baby's needs, you must also look after your own needs.

Time out
Make sure that you put aside a little time every day to relax and indulge yourself; it's in all the family's interest that you do.

Plan at least half an hour each day to devote entirely to yourself – you may want to have a bath, read a book, watch television, write a letter, meditate, exercise, listen to music, manicure your nails or give yourself a facial. Before the baby arrives, finding half an hour for yourself seems simple, but once she is born it can seem like an impossible task.

If you are to make some space for yourself, the first thing you must do is learn to accept offers of help graciously. Too many mothers feel they are failures if they don't personally attend to their child's every need. This can be a dangerous route to go down. It is based on unrealistic expectations and eventually leads to nervous exhaustion or even breakdown.

GETTING AWAY

If you and your partner have already discussed how you will share the new workload, the next stage is discussing how you can make some time for each other once the baby has arrived. Try to arrange for a baby-sitter to come at least once a month, or better still once a week, so that parenting doesn't take over every single waking second of your lives.

Look into the possibilities of nanny sharing (see column, p. 63) or, if you are not working full-time, see if you can arrange a "baby-swop" with another mother. You could also find out about courses or activities that offer a crèche. This is an ideal way to meet friends, take up an interest or increase your qualifications while your child is cared for and socializes with other children of her own age.

Spending time apart from your child doesn't necessarily make you a worse parent – in fact, in most cases it makes you a better one. If you spend all of your time with your child, she'll develop unrealistic expectations of relationships in general, and is likely to become overly demanding of friends and teachers alike.

Moreover, although your child needs to have a close and loving relationship with you, it is a big mistake to think that she needs your company every second of the day. She will gain confidence and acquire valuable social skills by learning how to interact with adults and other children.

EQUAL PARENTING

Almost nine out of ten women will not receive equal help from their partners. This is damaging for women and also very limiting for men.

A father's relationship with his partner may suffer if she feels resentment because of lack of help and support.

If a father doesn't play an active role in the early months and years of his baby's life, he may lose the chance to form a close childhood bond with his son or daughter.

A detached father will have a negative effect on his child. Girls may have trouble interacting with men, and boys will have no male role model.

Handing over
Your baby doesn't need you every minute of the day, so let someone else take care of her now and then while you go out.

SHOPPING WITH YOUR TODDLER

Once your child can walk, losing her in a crowd can be a worry, so take precautions against this.

- *Use reins or a wrist strap in busy places so she can't wander.*

- *Dress your toddler in something brightly coloured so that you can easily spot her from a distance.*

- *Have some sort of family code for your children to come back to you. I used to carry a small whistle around my neck.*

- *All shopping trips can be lessons even if you only teach your child about healthy eating (fresh vegetables are better than tinned ones, for example).*

- *From as early an age as possible, make your child learn her name, address and telephone number so that she can repeat them if she gets lost.*

- *Teach her never to walk off with any stranger.*

- *Make sure your child recognizes her surroundings when she's near to home by pointing out landmarks on every journey: "There's the pillar-box on the corner, and there's the blue gate, and our house is the next one along."*

TRAVEL AND OUTINGS

Time spent in planning your outing or travel schedule is never wasted. Be easy on yourself; try to take a friend or your partner with you if you can, so there is always an extra pair of hands and someone to help you, should you get into a scrape. Your baby can go with you anywhere as long as you're well enough prepared and have something in which to carry her – a sling, pushchair or car seat.

USING A PUSHCHAIR

You must become adept at collapsing and opening the pushchair within a few seconds without any problems, so practise it at home before your first outing. If you can't fold up the pushchair efficiently, you will find people jostling to get in front of you when you are in a queue, which will only add to your frustration. At the very least, you should be able to open it with only one hand, kick it shut with your feet and know how to operate the brakes – and don't forget you will have to do all these things while holding your child or preventing her from wandering off. Here are a few safety tips:

- When you open your pushchair, always make sure that it is in the fully extended position with the brakes fully and securely locked.
- Never put your child in the pushchair without securing the safety harness.
- Never, ever, leave your child in a pushchair unattended.
- Should your child fall asleep in the pushchair, adjust it to the lie-back position so that she can sleep comfortably.
- Don't put shopping on the handles of the pushchair; it can unbalance the pushchair and your child may be injured if it topples over.
- When you stop, always put the brakes on because you could inadvertently take your hands off the pushchair and it could run away.
- Check your pushchair regularly to make sure the brakes and catches work well and that the wheels are solid.

PUBLIC TRANSPORT

Always prepare yourself well ahead of time. I simply would not leave home with my children without some distracting toys, a favourite book and a favourite snack. All your belongings, including the pushchair, should be collected together prior to leaving and in good enough time so that you can check them over to make sure that you have not forgotten anything. The same goes for when you are getting off a bus or train; be ready to get off in plenty of time for your stop. Always ask for help from fellow passengers.

SPECIAL OUTINGS

When planning an outing for an older child, always try to consider what your child's personality can cope with best. If you have a quiet child who has a long concentration span, you can take her to a flower show or an antiques market, and point out the things around her. If, on the other hand, she is very active, she will need more space to run around in and a trip to the zoo, a playground or a fair is therefore more appropriate. Wherever you go, you should be prepared to make endless stops to look at anything that catches your child's attention. Always take enough drinks and snacks to keep your child happy for the full duration of the trip.

SHOPPING TRIPS

Taking a child shopping brings its own problems. Your toddler can easily become bored, hungry, fretful and difficult to manage, so it's worth planning ahead quite carefully to minimize stress. Taking a car will make a world of difference: you can feed and change your child in it, if necessary, stack your shopping in the boot and not have to carry it, and you won't have to worry about catching buses and trains. Try to shop fairly early in the day, because the streets and shops are less busy, and there are fewer distractions for your child. Always try to give your child a good, filling meal before you go out on a shopping trip; that way you may have several hours to complete your purchases without her getting hungry.

Bring whatever equipment you would take on any other trip. Bring some kind of small snack, too, because shopping seems to make children either hungry or fretful, and a snack will deal with both.

Handling a pushchair
Make sure that you can kick it shut, open it up one-handed and operate the brakes.

*On any kind of outing with
your child, the essential thing
is to plan and prepare well in
advance. These tips will all
help to make things go more
smoothly for you:*

• *Try to start travelling early
in the morning, or at night
when the roads are empty.*

• *Carry a bag of spare clothes
for each child in the car, be
philosophical about accidents
and change your child readily
into dry clothes.*

• *For safety, tape cutlery to
the inside of food containers.*

• *Always take some soft
clothing, such as an anorak or
a cotton sweater, that your
child can use as a pillow.*

• *Always have a supply of bags
into which cartons, bottles and
food wrappers can be placed
after use.*

• *Take a box of baby wipes to
clean dirty hands and faces.*

CONTROLLING YOUR TODDLER

Your young child will love being involved in shopping decisions, and she will feel very important and needed if you act on her preferences. With items where brand is not important to you, ask your child to select products by pointing to the one she would like you to buy. As my children got older and could toddle around the shopping trolley, I used to ask them to put all their choices into the shopping trolley themselves, so that they were constantly engaged looking for their favourite things, feeling a great sense of pride in finally finding them, and a sense of achievement in filling up the trolley. At the checkout don't feel that you have to pay for everything; without your child's seeing, you can take out those things you don't want.

One of the ways I used to distract and entertain my children on a shopping trip was to ask them if they were thirsty or hungry immediately on entering the supermarket, and get them a drink or a healthy snack. That way they could munch or sip their way around the supermarket and feel quite happy and occupied the whole time. If, however, you have a wayward child who keeps on getting into mischief, the only way to handle the situation is to keep your child on reins or a wrist strap to prevent her from wandering off and bothering other shoppers or getting lost.

Reins are a very good idea for an older child, because she will feel a sense of freedom and independence, but she will never be able to get very far away from you; a wrist link that is securely attached to her reins will prevent her becoming separated from you.

CAR JOURNEYS

Toddlers can be very active on car journeys. They're learning and taking great pride in newly acquired physical skills, like jumping, skipping, hopping, climbing and running, and it's very difficult for them to be confined in a small space. All this is intensified in hot weather because your child will become tired, touchy and tearful more easily than when the temperature is equable. Never leave a child alone in a car in hot weather, since the temperature inside the car can rise much higher than the temperature outside, causing her to become quickly overheated and even dehydrated. You should always screen your child from bright sunlight by putting a purpose-made blind over the window through which the sun is shining. You might also think about attaching a canopy to your child's seat, which serves the same purpose.

SAFETY IN THE CAR

Whatever the other considerations, when she is travelling in a car your child must be safe, and by law you must use some form of child restraint. Never sit in the front of a car with an unrestrained child, because if the car stops suddenly she will be flung out of your arms and will certainly be injured. A front-facing car seat is suitable for older babies and toddlers. After any accident, you should replace your seat belts, your child's car seat and the anchorage kit, since they will have been badly strained and may be damaged. For the same reason, you should never buy second-hand car seats, harnesses or anchorage kits.

Keeping your child happy Your child will get bored and hungry, so always have some nutritious snacks like raisins, sugarless cornflakes or pieces of cheese in plastic bags, and take more drinks than you ever think you'll need – your child's capacity for liquid is greatly increased on journeys. Seedless grapes make a very useful snack, because they quench your child's thirst as well as satisfying her hunger.

You'll need toys to distract your child while travelling (books may be a bad idea, however, if she suffers from motion sickness), and these can be arranged in different ways for safety and convenience. Buy or make a special cover for the front headrest of your car with pockets in the back that can carry drinks, snacks and toys, or tie toys to coat-hooks or handles so that they don't get lost under seats. Magnetized games are particularly useful in cars because the bits can't get lost, and you can stick Velcro on certain toys so that they will adhere to the car seat and stay in one place while your child is playing with them. I always found it best if I allowed my child to choose some of the toys that he wanted to take, and to be responsible for putting them into his own case or bag.

Cassettes with music or children's stories may give you at least half an hour of peace, so always have one at the ready. "I spy" games are always a favourite, particularly if you join in, and will keep your child occupied for quite a long time if you make the object interesting. Keep a special treat tucked away in the glove compartment with which to relieve tension or tears.

MOTION SICKNESS

If you have suffered motion sickness, or there's any family history of the condition, then your child is quite likely to suffer from motion sickness too. There are some things that you can do to help minimize it.

- *Don't give your child a rich or greasy meal before a journey.*

- *Use a motion-sickness drug, available from doctors; always give it to your child at least half an hour before you leave.*

- *Stay calm. If you're anxious your child will become anxious too. Car sickness is brought on by anxiety and excitement and is much more likely to happen on the outward journey, so be patient when you leave home.*

- *Snacks that can be sucked are a good idea, because they do not create a mess, so take along a supply of glucose sweets.*

- *Keeping your child occupied or distracted will help prevent car sickness, but don't let her read, since this may bring it on.*

If you notice your child becoming pale or quiet, ask her if she wants to stop. Get her to close her eyes until you reach a safe place to stop, then get her out of the car, and be very sympathetic if she actually is sick. Give her a short time to recover before you continue with your journey. Give your child a drink after she's been sick to get rid of the taste of vomit from her mouth.

CHILD CARE AND WORK

In the UK, you must go back to your job by the time the baby is 29 weeks old or your employer is no longer obliged to keep your job open for you. When it's time for you to return to work you may realize that you have not given yourself enough time to re-adjust after pregnancy. It is always a good idea to consult your doctor, since she or he can advise you about various health factors to consider. Some mothers find that they cannot bring themselves to leave the baby, while others – even though they adore the baby – are climbing the walls and have to "escape".

If you've decided to return to work, be assured that as long as you arrange good child care (see right), you won't be neglecting your child. There is no danger of your young baby forgetting who you are, or transferring her affection to her daytime carer. The really important thing is that when you get home you spend quality time with your child.

I know from my own experience as a working mother that guilt pangs are inevitable. I felt sure, however, that my baby would instinctively know I was his mother. I was reassured when I later came across research showing that very young babies are quite able to single out their parents (whether biological or adoptive) due to the loving, interested attention that only parents can give. Similarly, it has been shown that premature babies can distinguish between the touch of their parents' hands through an incubator and the more matter-of-fact handling of nursing staff. The important point is that it is the quality of the time you spend that counts more than the quantity. Love isn't measured in time: love is what you put into time, no matter how short it is.

GOING BACK TO WORK

The job you face at home is twice as demanding as any you would face at work, and your terms of employment at home are worse. After all, you are expected to work seven days a week, 365 days a year. You will be frowned upon if you don't cook, clean, wash, iron, entertain and provide advice, nursing care and sympathy continuously for at least 18 years, if not indefinitely. Your efforts will go largely unnoticed by society and, of course, you won't get paid a penny for the job. In fact you will have to pay for

Childminders
You will be able to tell from your child's reaction whether she feels loved and secure with her childminder.

the privilege of being a parent – but as the majority of parents will tell you, despite the terrible job description, it's a privilege worth paying for!

Your child's first step, first smile and first word are all priceless personal achievements. Helping to mould a tiny baby into a thoughtful, well-adjusted person is a task requiring sacrifice, responsibility and, above all, love. It also yields huge emotional dividends. To my mind, this makes parenting one of the most important and rewarding jobs in the world. Given this, it is disturbing to see the low status attached to parenting, particularly for women, who shoulder much of the burden. Being a good parent involves helping your child's personality to develop in a positive sense, and being a good role-model. If you want your children to grow up and work hard, then the fact that you work hard at your own job sets them an excellent example.

Having to combine the role of principal parent with full-time career is not easy, but women are doing it with imagination and sheer hard work. The rise of the mythical "super-mum" has meant that we are often expected to do it all without any help. There *are* a lot of "super-mums" around: they are the ones who manage everything day after day, at home and in the office, without failing to give love and energy to their children.

You should start looking for reliable child care about six weeks before you plan to return to work. Currently most governments don't give sufficient priority to providing child-care schemes for women, which makes things more difficult. Unfortunately, Britain has fewer nursery places for preschool children than any other country in Europe except Portugal. Nonetheless, things are gradually changing, for example, some companies now provide crèche schemes.

TODDLER EDUCATION

The choice as to whether or not you decide to send your child to preschool will depend largely upon the options available and whether or not they suit her needs. Find out what's available in your area and spend what time you can visiting nursery schools and talking to teachers and other parents so as to get a good idea of what is being provided.

There is no single kind of preschool that is best for every child. Each child should be in a school that fits her particular needs. All evaluations of preschool education show mixed results. One long-term assessment showed that

CHOOSING A CARER

Your baby doesn't only need to be changed and fed: she needs the kind of loving attention that you would give her yourself if she is to learn to interact and become a sociable child.

Childminders *These are usually mothers themselves, and must by law be registered with the local Social Services department. Your local council will provide a list, but you arrange payment and hours with the childminder.*

Day nurseries *Run privately or by local authorities, these often have long waiting lists and usually only a small number of places for babies. You may get priority if you are a single parent.*

Nanny or mother's help *This kind of help can be expensive, but you might consider sharing a nanny with another family. You can find a nanny through agencies, or by advertising locally or in a newspaper or magazine. Parents' groups may be able to put you in touch with other mothers interested in sharing a nanny.*

Crèche *Perhaps you are very lucky and have an enlightened employer who makes it possible to take your baby to work with you. This means you can continue breastfeeding and have your baby close by all day. If there's a crèche at your workplace, make sure that you arrange a place well before your baby is born.*

CHOOSING A NURSERY

When she's three or four your child will be able to go to nursery school, if you choose. Whether you feel this is the correct step will depend largely on her nature. For example, is she still shy and clinging or naturally outgoing? Only you can know whether she is ready.

Before making a decision, visit several nursery schools in your area. Prepare a checklist of important points so you don't forget any of them. For example, are the teachers relaxed or formal? Is it a happy environment? What is the standard of facilities? How many children are there, and are they well supervised? What subjects are taught? Does the school feel safe? Are the children happy?

You should sit in on a few classes and spend a whole morning or afternoon at the nursery school, and also speak to mothers whose children already attend. You will then have all the information you need to decide.

boys in Montessori programmes sustained gains in reading and maths throughout their school careers. Other research shows that children improve intellectually in all but the poorest of programmes. But it's difficult to know how long these benefits last. Evaluations of Head Start, an American-based preschool organization, for example, show that apparent IQ differences between children in Head Start and those who don't attend preschool diminish over time. Whatever the benefits of preschool education, there is no substitute for a loving and caring home environment.

Playgroups often take children from as early as two-and-a-half. They provide the opportunity for interaction with other children of the same age and help develop early social skills, but in a less formal atmosphere than nursery school.

Preschool has a number of benefits. Your child can develop greater confidence and therefore more self-control, as well as learning to share, to be concerned for the needs of others and to take turns. Her skill in planning ahead and co-operating with others will improve through fantasy and group play. The opportunities for play in preschool enhance the various ways that your child thinks – that is, imaginatively, speculatively and inventively. Some preschools are designed to help disadvantaged children by boosting their confidence. Children who attend such schools are less likely to repeat a year than their peers who did not attend preschool, less in need of special education and less likely to show delinquent behaviour when they reach adolescence.

I think there are very few risks to your child attending preschool, certainly no more than when she ventures outside the family; she'll just encounter them sooner. Risks may include minor health problems or exposure to behaviour you find objectionable, such as swearing and rude stories.

SETTLING IN AT PRESCHOOL

You can help your child adjust to nursery school by taking her along for one or two visits well in advance of her start date. Encourage her to play with the other children, and to sit at one of the desks or play with some of the equipment. But try not to push her to socialize with other children if she doesn't seem keen at first. Some children are naturally more gregarious than others and she will adjust in her own good time. The aim is to make her visits as enjoyable as possible. If you stress all the fun things she will do, her eager anticipation for school will be stronger than her worry about leaving you. If she is having trouble adjusting, most nursery schools will let you stay with her on the first day, and for steadily decreasing periods of time on the following days. Make sure you collect her yourself for the first week when she is most insecure. Once she is confident that she's not being abandoned, you'll be free to make other arrangements for collection.

Your child's personality, maturity, place in the family and willingness to leave home will all influence the way she settles down at preschool. In general, boys are more likely than girls of the same age to cry when their mothers first leave them at nursery school and they tend to cry when frustrated or angry with a teacher or helper. On the other hand, your child may enjoy being with other children as much as she enjoys the play and activities at preschool.

Although your child is now attending nursery school, this doesn't mean that your part in her education is finished. Ask her what she has done at the nursery school and who she played with. By getting her to talk over her school experiences you will be consolidating the new words and skills she is learning. You can help her to improve her use of language by repeating what she says in the correct form, although not by directly correcting her. Your child will be constantly seeking new information and you should always try to answer her questions truthfully. If you don't know the answer it is best to suggest you both look it up in a book, or ask daddy whether he knows, rather than just try to fob her off.

BEHAVIOUR AT NURSERY SCHOOL

As a rule, boys are more task-oriented in nursery school play and little girls talk more about being friends, recognizing similarities in each other, admiring one another's clothes, discussing who's friends with whom and so on.

A child's popularity at preschool fluctuates from day to day. Although intelligence and the ability to get along with others are just as important to popularity as a boy's size or physical prowess, dominant and aggressive behaviour in little boys is very much in evidence in a preschool setting. Hitting is a common form of aggressiveness, for example. A few girls strike out at other girls, but their hitting is usually not effective. Boys take longer to learn not to hit others and will make unprovoked – if rather mild – attacks on girls. It's not unusual, for example, for boys to push little girls or gesture menacingly at them.

PRESCHOOL EDUCATION

No single method of preschool has proved to be significantly better for every child. Many parents send their children to preschool to give them an opportunity to play and be sociable – others simply because it allows their children physical outlets that won't damage the furniture.

Structured classes are better suited to the needs of most small children. A chaotic environment may cause some boys to react in a way that some teachers describe as hyperactive. Structures vary within preschools. Some nursery schools follow a timetable for certain activities each day along the lines advocated by Dr Montessori, and organize the school around an orderly child-sized environment with specific behavioural guidelines, for example, putting things away when they are finished with.

A child who finds tasks easy and has plenty of local friends may be suited to a more traditional preschool. However, a child who has few local playmates and wants to socialize may enjoy a less structured preschool.

IF YOU SEPARATE

At some stage in every relationship, problems arise. In rare cases couples live happily ever after but the vast majority don't. This doesn't necessarily reflect a lowering of moral values; it is more an indication of the ever-increasing complexities and pressures of modern life. Support systems are weaker and expectations higher.

Statistics show that today two in three divorces are initiated by women, many of whom feel that they are asked to do too much without getting adequate support from their partners. The average marriage lasts eight years – a depressing fact of life for increasing numbers of children brought up without two parents.

PERIODS OF CHANGE

The problem for nearly all couples is that in the long term people change. Although this can be difficult, it can also be invigorating and constructive. If you learn to develop and grow together, you will prevent boredom and stagnation building up in your relationship.

At the end of periods of change, which are often fraught with emotional insecurity, you will either grow together or grow apart. Whatever happens, it is vital that your children feel secure of their future at all times. For young children, change within a family unit – or fear of that change – is very damaging. Children do not have the defence mechanisms to protect themselves from the severe emotional insecurity that a breakup can cause.

EXPLAINING TO YOUR CHILDREN

A young child is like a sponge that soaks up emotional signals, whether or not they are directed towards her. If you are happy, the chances are your child will be happy too; if you are sad, she will also be sad. Although it is always worth making an effort "for the sake of the children", don't fall into the trap of thinking they won't know what is going on. They usually sense when something is wrong, whether or not you have a smile on your face.

Because of this it's always best to explain, at least partially, what is going on. If you don't, children will invent their own explanations, mistakenly blaming themselves for problems in the family. This is because children under five conceive the world only in relation to themselves. If you don't give a plausible explanation of why you and your partner are arguing or splitting up, they may come up with explanations that are inconceivable to an adult but make perfect sense to a child, such as: "Daddy has left because I don't clean my room properly" or "Mummy is upset because I wet the bed/I'm clumsy/I lost my pocket money".

Feelings of guilt are severely damaging, especially for a child already struggling to come to terms with the emotional turmoil and insecurity that marital breakups can trigger. Doubt is one of the worst fears in a child's mind, so never leave your child in any doubt that you love her and that you will continue to look after her, even if you and your partner do separate.

DIVORCE

If you reach the point where the only option left is divorce or separation, do not assume automatically that your children will be devastated. Some will be, but the effect on your child will depend greatly on age, personality, the circumstances of the divorce and the prevailing social attitudes in the school and community.

I know of one primary school class in London, for instance, where out of 35 children, only five had parents who were still together. They were regularly teased by the others from "broken homes" who saw these five children as materially disadvantaged: the children whose parents were still together got only one set of presents on their birthday or at Christmas, and they had only one house.

Although having divorced or separated parents is nothing to boast about, many of the children in this class did. This may be deeply shocking to a lot of people, but it is just one more indication of the different times in which our children are growing up.

MOVING OUT

If the time comes when you have to leave, it is vital to let your child know that you are not taking your love with you, and that you will continue to be an active parent. Let your child know specifically when you plan to see her and, no matter how difficult it is, try never to break these arrangements, especially at the last minute.

If you are the parent left with full-time responsibility for your child when your partner has moved out, try not to be upset if she misses her father or mother. Don't try to make

THE EFFECT ON YOUR CHILDREN

A study suggests that children are better off with two unhappy parents than with divorced parents.

However, the research gives no indication of the different divorce situations that are critical in determining the effect on the children. An amicable divorce may be barely damaging and its effect entirely different from that of a bitter, acrimonious divorce. The main reason for this is that in an acrimonious situation, each parent usually does his or her best to turn the children against the other parent. This has a very negative and damaging effect on children, and should be avoided at all costs.

ACCESS

Whatever your feelings are about your partner, it's best for your child if you're easy-going and generous about giving your partner access.

Don't be stingy and don't be confrontational – it causes your child such anguish. Hand her over somewhere civilized like one of your homes, not somewhere like a park or shopping mall, or your child will feel like a commodity.

Plan well ahead, don't break promises at the last minute, and if your partner is late be breezy about it, otherwise your child will worry about both of you. Don't make it an opportunity to denigrate her father or mother; be offhand, and keep your child calm: "Oh, I expect the traffic's bad" or "Shall we have a game of snap till he gets here?".

If your partner is consistently late or unreasonable, arrange a separate meeting to discuss this, out of earshot of your child. The only time to consider preventing your ex-partner having any access to your child is if you think she's at risk of being kidnapped or otherwise harmed. In such cases it is best to seek professional advice, either through counselling services or a lawyer.

her forget that the other parent exists, and don't speak abusively or acrimoniously about the other parent since this will only confuse your child further.

Even if your child appears to be unaffected by a marital split, keep a close eye on her and ask her teachers if they notice any difference in her behaviour at school. Some children have fewer questions than others and keep their feelings of insecurity to themselves, but they may still need extra attention and love. Increased bedwetting, thumb-sucking and general "clinginess" are all signs that your child is in need of reassurance and special care.

Grandparents can be a great boon at the time of the divorce. If possible, do encourage your child to see both sets. Don't let bad feeling act as a cut-off. Think of your child first – she needs continuity, security and reassurance, and grandparents are second to none at providing these as long as they don't bad-mouth either parent. Grandparents will also act as a mainstay during access periods and will show your child the unconditional love that every child needs if their parents are divorcing or separating.

Ask your children about their worries and anxieties and give them space to voice them. Listen and take their concerns seriously. Act upon them. They will almost certainly be things of which you haven't thought, or would dismiss as trivial if you did.

CHAPTER 4

A TODDLER'S HEALTH

Most parents know when their child is sickening for
something, even though it's difficult to know what precisely
is wrong. This chapter will help you decide when to call the
doctor, when home nursing will suffice and what to do to
make your child comfortable. A child may need special care
and attention because of a chronic condition, such as
asthma, a learning disorder, such as dyslexia, or he may
simply be very advanced for his years. Early identification of
special needs is very important; you are your child's main
caregiver, and the better informed you are, the more you can
do for him. First aid is an essential skill for all parents.

TAKING YOUR CHILD'S PULSE

The average pulse rate for a one-year-old child is 100–120 beats per minute. This slows to 80–90 for a seven-year-old child.

In a child over one year, it should be relatively easy to find the pulse on his wrist. Use your middle and index fingers, not your thumb, since it contains a pulse of its own. Place your two fingers on the spot on your child's wrist immediately below his thumb. Count the number of beats over a 15-second period and then multiply this figure by four to get the pulse rate per minute.

WHEN YOUR CHILD IS ILL

It's fairly easy to recognize when your child is ill: he'll be pale, listless and off his food. You should be able to treat him successfully at home for most things. If you're ever worried or in two minds, however, call your doctor. Some situations always require immediate medical attention (see Emergencies, opposite).

WHEN TO CALL THE DOCTOR

It is usually apparent when your child is falling ill, and signs that you should monitor closely are your child's temperature, appetite and breathing rate.

Raised temperature The normal body temperature for a child is 37°C (98.6°F). When your child's temperature rises above 38°C (100.4°F) he has a fever, in which case you should seek medical help. Consult a doctor urgently if a raised temperature is accompanied by a stiff neck and a rash, since these symptoms may indicate meningitis (see p. 79).

Diarrhoea Loose, watery bowel movements mean that the intestines are inflamed and irritable; the most common cause is gastroenteritis. Diarrhoea is always serious in babies and young children since it can lead to dehydration.

Vomiting You should consult your doctor if your child has been vomiting intermittently during a six-hour period or longer, especially if the vomiting is accompanied by diarrhoea or fever. Vomiting is usually caused by food that does not suit or gastroenteritis. Occasionally, there may be a more serious cause; your doctor will make a diagnosis.

Pain You should see your doctor if your child complains of headaches, particularly after he's bumped his head or if the headache comes on a few hours after the head injury, or if there is blurred vision, nausea, dizziness or stomach pain, particularly on the lower right side of the abdomen.

Breathing Difficulty in breathing is a medical emergency and requires immediate help. Breathing may be laboured and you may notice that your child's ribs are drawn in sharply each time he takes a breath. If your child's lips go blue you should treat this as an emergency and send for an ambulance (see Call an ambulance, p. 89).

Appetite Sudden changes in appetite may indicate underlying illness, especially if your child has a fever, even a mild one. Your doctor should be alerted if your child refuses food for a day and seems lethargic.

WHAT TO TELL YOUR DOCTOR

In order to make a diagnosis your doctor will need: a description of your child's symptoms; when they started; in what order they occurred; how severe they are; and whether anything precipitated them (eating something poisonous, for instance). In addition to this, your doctor will need to know your child's age and medical history.

The specific questions your doctor may ask about an illness are: Has your child vomited or had diarrhoea? Does he have any pain? Where is it? How long has it lasted? Have you given him anything for it? Is his temperature raised? How quickly did the fever come on and what was his highest temperature? Has he lost consciousness at any time? Have you noticed swollen glands or a rash? Has he had any dizziness or blurred vision? The doctor will also ask general questions about your child's appetite and sleeping patterns.

What to ask your doctor If your child is prescribed drugs, make sure that you know when they should be taken (some need to be taken on a full or empty stomach), how long they should be taken for and whether there are likely to be any side-effects. Find out how your child should be nursed and how soon his symptoms can be expected to go away.

EMERGENCIES

You should call an ambulance or take your child to the nearest casualty department by car should any of the following potentially life-threatening situations happen:

• A bone fracture or suspected fracture.
• A severe reaction (such as red blotchy skin or wheezing) to a sting or bite from an insect or animal.
• Pale blue or grey skin around the lips and under the fingernails.
• A burn or scald (from a wet or dry source) that is larger than the area of your child's hand.
• Poisoning or suspected poisoning.
• Unconsciousness.
• Severe bleeding from a wound.
• Contact with a corrosive chemical (such as bleach or weedkiller), especially involving the eyes.
• Laboured breathing or choking.
• Any injuries to the ears or eyes.
• An electric shock.
• Inhalation of toxic fumes such as smoke or gas.

THERMOMETERS

Mercury thermometers, in which a narrow column of mercury expands in response to heat and moves up to a point on a calibrated scale, are the most accurate.

Take the reading under the armpit. Place the thermometer bulb in your child's armpit and fold his arm over his chest; hold in place for about three minutes. Bear in mind that the temperature reading in the armpit is 0.6°C (1°F) below actual body temperature.

Other types of thermometer include liquid crystal (strip) and digital thermometers.

Strip thermometers are less accurate than others, but simple to use. You just hold the thermometer against your child's forehead for a minute or so; a glowing panel indicates the temperature reading.

Digital thermometers show the temperature reading in a window. They're accurate and unbreakable, but more expensive than other kinds.

Don't put a mercury thermometer in your child's mouth until he's at least seven.

GENERAL NURSING

As well as the treatment your doctor recommends, the following routines will help your child to feel more comfortable while he's ill:

- *Air your child's room and bed at least once a day.*

- *Leave a bowl by your child's bed if he is vomiting or has whooping cough.*

- *Leave a box of tissues by your child's bed.*

- *Give small meals frequently; your child may find large portions off-putting.*

- *Don't insist that your child eats if he doesn't feel like it, but do encourage him to drink lots of fluids.*

- *Sponge your child down with tepid water if he has a fever.*

- *Give liquid paracetamol for pain relief.*

NURSING YOUR CHILD

You don't need any special skills or medical knowledge to look after your sick child. It helps if you relax the rules and try to hide your anxiety from him.

IN BED OR NOT?

At the beginning of an illness when your child is feeling quite poorly he will probably want to stay in bed and he may sleep a lot. As he starts to feel better he will still need bed rest, but he will want to be around you and he may want intervals of playing. The best way to accommodate this is to make up a bed on the sofa in a room near where you are working so that he can lie down when he wants to. Don't insist that your child goes to bed just because he is ill – children with a fever, for instance, don't recover faster if they stay in bed. When your child is tired, however, it is time to put him to bed. But don't just leave him alone. Make sure that you visit him at regular intervals (every half an hour), and find the time to stay and play a game, read a book or do a puzzle.

GIVING DRINKS

It is essential that your child drinks a lot when he's ill – when he has a fever, diarrhoea or is vomiting – because he will be dehydrated and need to replace lost fluids. The recommended fluid intake for a child with a fever is 100–150 millilitres per kilogram (1½ – 2½ fluid ounces per pound) of body weight per day, which is the equivalent of 1 litre (2 pints) per day for a child who weighs 9 kilograms (20 pounds).

Encourage your child to drink by leaving his favourite drink at his bedside (preferably not sugary, fizzy drinks such as cola), by putting drinks in glasses that are especially appealing and by giving him bendy straws to drink with.

KEEPING YOUR CHILD OCCUPIED

Illness is an occasion when you can completely indulge your child. When he is not resting, spend time playing games and talking to him. Relax all the rules and let him play whatever games he wants to, even if you've previously not allowed them in bed. If your child wants to do something messy like painting, just spread an old sheet or a sheet of polythene over the bed. If you can, move a television into his room temporarily – this will keep him entertained and make him feel special as well.

Let him do some painting; read aloud to him; get out some of his old toys and play with them together; buy him small presents and let him unwrap them; sing songs or make up a story together; ask him to draw a picture of what he is going to do when he feels better; and, unless he has an infectious illness, let some friends visit him for a brief period during the day. As your child gets better let him play outside, but if he has a fever discourage him from running around too much.

VOMITING

Your child will probably find vomiting a distressing experience and you should try to make him as comfortable as possible. Get him to sit up in bed and make sure there is a bowl or a bucket within easy reach, so that he doesn't have to run to the toilet. When he's being sick hold his head and comfort him (with girls, tie back long hair). Afterwards help your child to clean his teeth, or give him a peppermint to suck to take the taste away.

When your child hasn't vomited for a few hours and he's feeling hungry, offer him bland foods, like mashed potato, but don't encourage him to eat if he doesn't want to. More important than eating is maintaining a constant level of fluids. Provide lots of water, and add a half teaspoon of salt and four teaspoons of glucose per 500 millilitres (1 pint) to replace lost salts and minerals. Avoid drinks such as milk, and give him plenty of fruit juice diluted with water.

TREATING A HIGH TEMPERATURE

Call your doctor if the fever lasts more than 24 hours or if there are any accompanying symptoms like vomiting or a rash. (Temperatures over 38°C (100.4°F) should be taken seriously in all children.)

Cool your child down by taking his clothes off and getting him to lie on the bed. Sponge him all over with tepid water and keep taking his temperature every minute until it has stabilized at 38°C (100.4°F). Never use cold water to sponge him since this causes the blood vessels to constrict and the temperature to increase. Cover him with a light cotton bedsheet and take his temperature every five minutes to check that it doesn't go up again. Changing the sheets on your child's bed regularly will help to keep him comfortable. It's still important for your child to drink lots of fluids since he will be perspiring a lot.

FEBRILE CONVULSIONS

The most common cause of convulsions in babies is a raised temperature that accompanies a viral infection. This sort of convulsion is most common in children between six months and four years, and is known as a febrile convulsion.

During a convulsion the muscles of the body twitch involuntarily due to a temporary abnormality in brain function. Possible symptoms include loss of consciousness, loss of bowel and bladder control, rhythmic jerking of the limbs, with sleepiness and confusion on coming round. You should clear a space around him so that he doesn't damage himself. Wait until his body has stopped jerking and then place him in the recovery position (see p. 90).

You'll need to sponge your child with tepid (never cold) water to reduce his temperature. Don't leave him alone, don't try to restrain him and don't put anything in his mouth. Call a doctor as soon as your child has come round. If the convulsion lasts more than 15 minutes, call an ambulance.

Treating Common Childhood Illnesses

Any illness in a child is different from, and more serious than, the same illness in an adult because the immune system is not fully developed. Getting familiar with the advice in these pages will help you to take prompt action if your child feels ill.

EARS

Ear infections are common in children because their Eustachian tubes (the tubes that connect the middle ear to the throat) are short, so any throat infection can ascend quickly to the middle ear.

MIDDLE EAR INFECTION

Otitis media or infection of the middle ear is quite common in children and is associated with recurrent tonsillitis. In fact, one of the main reasons for removing tonsils (and adenoids) is chronic middle ear infections. Infections are caused by bacteria entering the middle ear from the nose and the throat via the Eustachian tube. If middle ear infections are left untreated, they can result in permanent hearing loss. Recurrent middle ear infections are often linked with glue ear (see right).

Symptoms The most prominent symptoms are severe earache and loss of appetite. Your child may also have a fever or a discharge from the ear, and there may be some hearing loss. A toddler with a middle ear infection may be distressed and pull and rub the affected ear, which will be very red; in fact the whole side of his face may be inflamed.

Treatment The usual treatment is a course of antibiotics and pain-relieving medication. At home you should keep your child comfortable and cool and give lots of drinks as well as his medicines. An ear, nose and throat specialist should treat repeated middle ear infections to avoid glue ear, and in some cases an operation to remove the tonsils will be recommended.

GLUE EAR

If your child has repeated infections of the middle ear or throat, or tonsillitis, the middle ear can gradually fill with jelly-like fluid. Because the fluid cannot drain away through the Eustachian tube, it becomes glue-like and impairs hearing because the sounds are not being transmitted across the middle ear to the inner ear, where they are actually heard. It's important to deal with glue ear promptly or your child could be slow to speak and learn.

Symptoms Glue ear generally causes no pain, but partial hearing loss and a feeling of fullness deep in the ear may occur. A child with chronic glue ear may sleep with his mouth open, snore and speak with a nasal twang. If glue ear is not treated it can cause permanent deafness, resulting in speech and learning problems.

Treatment After examining your child's ear with an otoscope, a doctor may prescribe antibiotics to clear the infection and vasoconstrictor drugs to allow the fluid to drain. In severe or recurring cases of glue ear, a minor operation may be necessary to insert a grommet – a plastic tube that drains off the mucus through the eardrum, which quickly heals after the grommet drops out. Grommets quite often drop out of their own accord and rarely have to be reinserted since all the fluid has drained. A child who has grommets fitted should take precautions to avoid letting water into the ears, and should swim only if he is wearing snugly fitting earplugs.

THROAT

Throat infections such as tonsillitis and adenitis are rare in babies under one year. They are more common in children who have just started school and are being exposed to a new range of bacteria.

SORE THROAT

An uncomfortable or painful throat is usually due to infection by a bacterium such as streptococcus, or a virus such as the cold or flu viruses.

Symptoms Your child may tell you that he has a sore throat, or you may notice that he finds it hard to swallow. Depress his tongue with a spoon handle and tell him to say "aaahhh" so that you can look down his throat for signs of inflammation or enlarged red tonsils.

Treatment Give lots of drinks, and liquidize your child's food if he finds it difficult to swallow. Your doctor may prescribe an antibiotic if there is a bacterial infection or tonsillitis.

TONSILLITIS AND SWOLLEN ADENOIDS

The tonsils, situated on both sides of the back of the throat, prevent bacteria that invade the throat from entering the body by trapping and killing them. This can sometimes result in the tonsils themselves becoming swollen and infected. The adenoids, which are situated at the back of the nose, are nearly always affected at the same time.

Symptoms Your child will complain of a sore throat and may find swallowing difficult. On examination, the tonsils appear red and enlarged, possibly with yellow and white patches. He may have a raised temperature, the glands in his neck may be swollen and his breath might smell. If the adenoids are swollen, too, his speech may sound nasal.

Treatment Consult your doctor, who may take a throat swab and examine your child's ears and glands. Bacterial tonsillitis is treated with appropriate antibiotics. Removal of the tonsils is considered after many severe recurrent attacks, or if the ears are badly affected too.

SKIN

Childhood skin complaints may be caused by an infection, an allergy or a response to very high or low temperatures. Most of them are minor and can easily be treated. Rashes occur with a variety of complaints, some of which are serious; if you are at all worried about a rash, consult your doctor.

INFANTILE ECZEMA

This inflammatory skin condition is caused by an inherited tendency plus a trigger factor such as an allergy or an infection. Occasionally it is simply a response to stress. The type of eczema that usually affects children is atopic eczema. It appears between two and 18 months of age, typically occurring on the face, hands, neck and ankles and in the knee and elbow creases. Seborrhoeic dermatitis can also affect children. This occurs on the scalp, eyelids and ears, around the nose and in the ear canal and groin.

Symptoms Skin affected by atopic eczema is raw, dry, scaly, red and itchy, and there may be small white blisters, like grains of rice, which burst and weep if scratched. Seborrhoeic eczema looks similar to atopic eczema but is less itchy. Itchiness is the most irritating symptom of eczema, causing severe scratching and sleeplessness.

Treatment If you suspect your child has eczema see your doctor, who may prescribe an anti-inflammatory cream and anthistamines to curb itching and combat any allergy. If the skin has become infected, antibiotics may be necessary. Your doctor will also try to identify the cause of the eczema: a pet, washing powder or a particular food, for example.

Keep contact with water to a minimum, and if you have to bathe your child, put baby oil in the bath. Stop using soap, and make sure that clothes are thoroughly rinsed and contain no trace of washing powder or fabric conditioner. Minimize your child's contact with potential allergens, use emollient cream on his skin, and keep his fingernails short so that he cannot damage the skin by scratching. Use cotton fabrics, never wool.

COLDS AND COUGHS

Infections with cold or flu viruses are common in childhood because children have not yet developed immunity to specific viruses. There are roughly 200 cold viruses producing similar symptoms – your child will never get the same virus twice.

COMMON COLD

Colds are not serious unless your child is very young, or a complication such as bronchitis sets in. Colds are more frequent when your child starts nursery school, because he will suddenly be exposed to lots of new viruses.

Symptoms Most cold viruses start with "catarrhal" symptoms (blocked or runny nose, cough, sore throat), fever and listlessness. The nasal discharge is first clear and then thick and yellow as the body's defences take over. The rise in temperature that accompanies a cold can cause cold sores, hence their name.

Treatment Only symptoms can be treated, not the virus itself; there's no cure for the common cold. If a secondary infection such as sinusitis or bronchitis appears, then your doctor will prescribe antibiotics; otherwise, home remedies suffice. Give your child plenty of fluids, encourage him to blow his nose frequently, showing him how to clear one nostril at a time, and apply petroleum jelly to his nostrils and top lip if they become sore or chapped. When congestion is severe, make sure that he sleeps with his head propped up with pillows, and try applying a menthol rub to his chest. Your doctor will prescribe nose drops if a blocked nose interferes with sleeping or eating. Liquid paracetamol reduces the temperature and eases aches and pains.

COUGHS

The cough is a reflex action that clears the throat of any irritant such as mucus, food, dust or smoke. A cough may be due to the irritation of a cold, sore throat, tonsillitis or sinusitis. The cause should always be treated, not just the cough alone, since it is merely a symptom of an underlying condition.

Symptoms There are two types of cough: a productive cough, in which phlegm is produced, and a non-productive cough, in

Clearing the sinuses
Get your child to inhale dissolved menthol crystals in boiling water. Cover his head with a towel to keep in the menthol vapours.

which there is no phlegm. The first has a "wet" sound, while the second is dry and hacking. Both will prevent sleep. A cough may also be a nervous symptom. If a cough is hacking or croaking, your child may have croup – a condition in which the vocal cords become swollen and inflamed, usually as a result of an upper respiratory viral infection. Coughing can be so distressing as to cause vomiting.

Treatment If you suspect that your child has croup or asthma (see p. 85) you should seek medical help straight away. An underlying chronic infection like sinusitis or tonsillitis should be treated separately. Most other coughs can be treated at home as long as they don't stop your child from sleeping or eating.

Discourage your child from running around, since breathlessness may bring on a coughing fit, and get him to lie on his stomach or side at night; this prevents mucus running down the throat. Give your child plenty of warm drinks, and if he is coughing up lots of phlegm give him an expectorant medicine, and lay him over your lap and pat him on the back. Suppress a dry cough, but never try to suppress a productive cough.

INFECTIOUS DISEASES

An infectious disease is one that is caused by a micro-organism – that is, a bacterium or a virus. The infection is most commonly spread via the air or by direct contact, although it may also be spread via food, water or insects, particularly in poor conditions. In countries where standards of sanitation are high, appropriate drugs are readily available and health and nutrition are generally good, infectious diseases pose far less of a threat than they once did. In addition, many serious infectious diseases have been virtually eliminated in developed countries by immunization (see p. 80). The characteristics of many childhood infectious diseases are similar: a rash on the body, a fever, general malaise and common cold symptoms. If you notice a rash and your child's temperature is raised, tell your doctor. The dangers with most illnesses are that your child may become dehydrated from vomiting or refusing food and drink, have difficulty breathing due to constricted airways, or suffer febrile convulsions (see column, p. 73). Some diseases can lead to complications if left untreated.

CHICKENPOX
A common and mild viral disease.
Possible symptoms Red, itchy spots that become fluid-filled blisters and then scabs. Headache and slight fever.
Treatment Apply calamine lotion to the rash, keep your child at home and discourage scratching. Your doctor may prescribe an anti-infective cream.
Complications In very rare cases chickenpox may lead to encephalitis (inflammation of the brain) and, if aspirin is taken, Reye's syndrome, a serious illness whose symptoms are nausea, vomiting, noticeable lethargy and fever.

Applying lotion
The rash that accompanies chickenpox is very itchy. To soothe the itch, dab on calamine lotion; the spots may leave scars if they are scratched at all vigorously.

GERMAN MEASLES

A viral infection, usually mild in children.
Possible symptoms Small red spots, appearing first behind the ears, then spreading to the face and all over the body. Slight fever and enlarged lymph nodes at the back of the neck.
Treatment There is no specific medical treatment. You can give your child liquid paracetamol if he has a fever, and you should try to keep him in isolation.
Complications The biggest risk is to pregnant women who come into contact with a child with German measles, since it causes birth defects. There is a slight risk of encephalitis (inflammation of the brain).

MUMPS

A fairly common viral illness that is seldom serious in children.
Possible symptoms Tender, swollen glands below the ears and beneath the chin. Fever, headache, dry mouth and difficulty chewing and swallowing. Less common symptoms are painful testicles in boys and swollen ovaries in girls.
Treatment There is no specific medical treatment. Keep your child away from nursery, liquidize his food and make sure he has plenty of fluids, and give him liquid paracetamol for the pain and fever.
Complications Occasionally leads to meningitis, encephalitis and pancreatitis. In boys, occasionally, one of the testes is affected, and decreases in size. Infertility can result if both testes are affected, but this occurs very rarely.

MEASLES

A highly infectious and potentially serious viral illness.
Possible symptoms Brownish-red spots appear behind the ears and then spread to the rest of the body. White spots in the mouth (known as Koplik spots) are the diagnostic sign. The child is feverish, has a runny nose, a cough and a headache. He may have sore eyes and find it hard to tolerate bright lights.
Treatment Keep your child in bed for the duration of the fever, keep him away from school and give him liquid paracetamol and plenty of fluids. Your doctor may prescribe eye drops for sore eyes and antibiotics for secondary infections.
Complications Ear and chest infections, vomiting and diarrhoea may occur a couple of days after the appearance of the brownish-red spots. There is also a slight risk of pneumonia and encephalitis (inflammation of the brain). The lungs and ears may be permanently damaged if antibiotics aren't given.

WHOOPING COUGH

A bacterial infection that clogs the airways with mucus.
Possible symptoms A cough with a distinctive "whoop" sound as the child tries to breathe, common cold symptoms (see p. 76) and vomiting. Coughing may prevent your child from sleeping.
Treatment Your doctor may prescribe antibiotics, and in severe cases your child may need to go to hospital for oxygen therapy and treatment for dehydration. Encourage your child to bring up phlegm by laying him over your lap and patting his back as he coughs. Don't let him run around or exert himself, and keep him away from cigarette smoke.
Complications The main danger is dehydration due to persistent vomiting. Sometimes a severe attack of whooping cough can damage the lungs and make your child prone to chest infections. Secondary infections, which are rare, include pneumonia and bronchitis.

MENINGITIS

An inflammation of the membranes that cover the brain and spinal cord, resulting from a viral or bacterial infection. Epidemics of meningitis are caused by the meningococcus bacterium. The Hib vaccination (see p. 80) protects against this form, which is very serious.

Possible symptoms Fever, stiff neck, lethargy, headache, vomiting, intolerance of bright light and, in children under two, bulging fontanelle (the membranous gap between the bones in the skull). In meningococcal meningitis, a purple rash that doesn't disappear on pressure may cover most of the body. If a purple rash appears, press a drinking glass to the skin to see if it remains visible. If it does, your child should be taken straight to hospital.

Treatment Intravenous antibiotics are used to treat bacterial meningitis, and painkilling drugs relieve the symptoms of viral meningitis.

Complications Viral meningitis is not usually serious and clears up within a week. Bacterial meningitis is potentially fatal because of the risk of meningococcal septicaemia, and so should always be treated as a medical emergency.

DIPHTHERIA

A serious and highly contagious bacterial infection. It is now very rare because of widespread immunization.

Possible symptoms The tonsils are enlarged and may be covered by a grey membrane. Your child may have a mild fever, a cough, a sore throat, breathing difficulties and headaches.

Treatment Diphtheria is very serious because of the possibility of breathing difficulties, and your child should be hospitalized immediately. He will be given strong antibiotics and he may need

a tracheostomy to help him to breathe; this means that a small tube will be inserted into the windpipe to bypass the blockage in the throat.

Complications Pneumonia and heart failure, if the disease is not treated.

SCARLET FEVER

A bacterial infection whose effects are similar to those of tonsillitis (see p. 75), but accompanied by a rash. It is not very common, and rarely serious.

Possible symptoms Enlarged tonsils and a sore throat, a high temperature (up to 40°C or 104°F), abdominal pains, vomiting, a rash of small spots that starts on the chest then spreads and merges, but does not affect the mouth area, and a furry tongue with red patches.

Treatment Your doctor may prescribe antibiotics. Home treatment includes giving your child plenty of fluids and liquidizing food to make it easier to eat. Give liquid paracetamol to lower temperature.

Complications If your child is sensitive to the streptococcus bacterium it may cause complications, including nephritis (inflammation of the kidneys) and rheumatic fever (inflammation of the joints and heart). Both are rare.

Checking the throat
Use a spoon or spatula to hold your child's tongue down while you check his throat. Enlarged tonsils and a sore throat may be symptoms of scarlet fever.

IMMUNIZATION

There are two types of immunization: passive and active. The former works by introducing already-formed antibodies into the body. The latter involves injecting a weakened bacterium that encourages the body's immune system to produce its own antibodies – this is why immunization can sometimes produce mild symptoms of the disease it is intended to protect against.

In the first five years of your child's life, he will need several immunizations: three DTP injections, three polio immunizations (taken orally), one MMR injection and three Hib injections. Vaccines do not provide instant protection against disease; they take up to four weeks to be effective. Give liquid paracetamol to ease discomfort.

Immunization protects both individuals and whole communities from infectious diseases. Every child should therefore be properly immunized. Some mothers are alarmed by stories about the side-effects of vaccinations, but these are actually quite rare. Your child shouldn't be vaccinated, however, if he has a fever or infection, or if he's had a severe reaction to a previous dose of vaccine. Your doctor or health visitor will advise you.

PREVENTING TETANUS

There is a danger of tetanus with any deep wound. Tetanus bacteria and spores live in soil and manure, so dirty wounds are dangerous. The bacteria produce a poison that attacks the nerves and brain, causing muscle spasm, particularly of the face, hence the common name lockjaw. Patients always require treatment in hospital. Immunization prevents tetanus completely. The first tetanus injection should be given before 12 months, with boosters at ten-yearly intervals up to a total of five doses. If your child has a dog bite or a deep, dirty cut and has not been immunized, he must have a tetanus injection straight away at a casualty department.

IMMUNIZATION PROGRAMME

INJECTION	PROTECTS AGAINST	COMMENTS
DTP	Diphtheria, tetanus and pertussis (whooping cough)	Given as three injections at two, three and four months.
Polio	Polio	Given by mouth at two, three and four months. A booster dose is given at the age of five, and lasts for about ten years.
MMR	Measles, mumps and rubella	Given to babies at about 13 months, or any time after this, and offers lasting protection.
Hib	The bacterium *Haemophilus influenzae* type b (can cause bacterial meningitis, a severe form of croup, blood poisoning and other infections)	Given at two, three and four months.

YOUR CHILD IN HOSPITAL

If you don't like hospitals and you convey this negative attitude to your child, you may inadvertently make his stay in hospital more difficult than it has to be. Try to teach him that a hospital is a friendly place where people go to get better. Whenever the chance arises – if you have a friend or a relative in hospital, for instance – take your child along when you go to visit and be matter-of-fact, not gloomy, about their illness. If a child's first experience of a hospital is when he becomes sick, it will seem more alien than it would otherwise.

If you know that your child is going to hospital read him a story about a child who goes into hospital, and role play doctors and nurses with toy stethoscopes. Be as honest as you can about why he's going to hospital, and emphasize that it's to make him better. Reassure him that you will be with him as much as you can, and if he's old enough to understand, tell him when he'll be well enough to come home.

If your child requires an operation he'll probably be curious about what's going to happen to him. Answer his questions as honestly as you can – if he asks you whether the operation will hurt, don't pretend that it won't, but tell him that doctors have medicines to make the pain go away quickly.

WHAT TO TAKE

You can help your child prepare for a stay in hospital by packing a bag with him. One of the most unsettling things will be the unfamiliar surroundings and change of routine, so let him have some of his own things with him: a personal stereo and tapes or a radio, travel games, cuddly toys and a photograph for his bedside. For a short stay pack the following necessities:

- A toilet bag containing a hair brush, comb, soap, flannel, toothbrush and toothpaste.
- Three pairs of pyjamas or three nightdresses.
- A dressing gown and a pair of slippers.
- Three pairs of socks.
- Three pairs of pants.

IN HOSPITAL

Many hospitals allow parents to stay with their children 24 hours a day. Whether your hospital does or not, try to spend as much time as possible with your child, especially at first, when his surroundings are unfamiliar. Let him know when you are going to come, and always keep your promises about visiting. Ask the nurses on the ward whether you can bathe, change and feed your child. If he is well enough, you can read to him and play games with him. If you can't stay at the hospital all the time, encourage your partner, friends and relatives to visit at different times, rather than all together, so that your child has someone he knows well with him almost all the time.

COMING HOME

Depending on how long your child has been in hospital, you may notice some changes in his habits when he comes home. He probably woke up and went to sleep much earlier in hospital than he does at home, and these sleeping and waking patterns may carry on for a while. He may resent the discipline at home after having been spoiled and indulged a little, and he may be reluctant to go back to school. The best approach to these things is to be tolerant and patient, since your child will soon adapt to life at home again.

Children With Special Needs

Early identification of special needs is very important. Always seek professional advice if you are at all worried about your child.

UNDERACHIEVEMENT

Underachievers or developmentally delayed children acquire skills at an unusually slow rate. Some of the first indications that your child is "behind" are docility, quietness and sleeping for very long periods. Your baby will not make much noise, will not interact with his environment in the same way as the average child and will be late in smiling, responding to sounds, and learning to chew.

When you try to engage your child in activities he will have a short attention span, and he will spend brief periods doing lots of different things rather than devoting all his energy to one task or game. As he grows older he may demonstrate a tendency to be overactive and he may have a lower than average IQ.

DIAGNOSIS

A developmentally delayed child will be later than usual in achieving some of the important developmental milestones (see below). It is important, however, to eliminate the possibility that your child has a physiological problem such as partial deafness. You should also find out whether your child has a severe developmental disorder, such as dyslexia (see right), or whether he is just developing at a below-average rate. Ask your doctor to refer your child to a psychologist for assessment. Your child may need remedial help.

BEHAVIOURAL MILESTONES

Although children vary in the speed at which they develop, behavioural milestones do exist. If your child has not reached the following stages then he may have a learning or developmental disorder.

Hand regard Your baby becomes aware of his hands at about the age of eight weeks, shortly after he begins to play with his feet. Between the age of 12 and 16 weeks your baby will stare at his hands and waggle his fingers – he's discovering that he can control his hand movements. Hand regard may go on for as long as 20 weeks, however, in developmentally delayed children.

The grasp reflex If you put your finger (or any object) into a baby's palm he will close his fingers around it in a tight grip. This reflex usually lasts about six weeks after birth, but will persist longer if your child is developmentally delayed.

Mouthing At about six months your baby will put everything that he can into his mouth. This behaviour will last until around a year in a normal child and longer in a developmentally delayed child.

Casting Children up to the age of 16 months will throw objects out of their pram – a behaviour known as casting. Developmentally delayed children may continue to do this for much longer.

Dribbling Slobbering and dribbling should stop at around one year. Developmentally delayed children may still be dribbling at the age of 18 months.

HOW YOU CAN HELP

Intellectual development is determined by both nature (inherited qualities) and nurture (things such as physical and social environment, and diet). Your child's IQ is decided before birth, but it can flower through the stimuli that your child is exposed to after birth. If your child is not encouraged to interact with other people and to use his senses from an early age, the chances are that he will not reach his full potential, even if that potential is limited.

If you suspect that your child is lagging behind, spend lots of time reading aloud and talking to him, playing with him, taking him out, showing him new things and new people and encouraging him to play imaginative games with his toys. Give him toys that are educational and plenty of colourful books and pictures to look at.

Behaviour modification techniques may help. Put simply, this means rewarding your child's responses with praise and affection and being patient with his efforts, however slow they are. If you punish him for slowness, he may become discouraged and lose his incentive to learn.

DYSLEXIA

This is a learning disorder that affects reading, spelling and written language. These difficulties may be accompanied by problems with numbers, poor short-term memory and clumsiness. Although dyslexia particularly affects your child's mastery of written symbols – letters, numbers and musical notation – he may have difficulties with spoken language too. Dyslexia is a specific neurological disorder and is not the result of poor hearing or vision, or low intelligence. One in twenty children is dyslexic (three times more boys than girls), and if you or your partner is dyslexic then your child is 17 times more likely to suffer from the disorder.

DIAGNOSIS

Many bright children are dyslexic, and the condition is often diagnosed earlier in these children since parents become aware of the gap between their child's obvious intelligence and his level of achievement in specific areas. The main symptoms of dyslexia are difficulty in reading and writing. Your child may have problems perceiving letters in the correct order, or he may confuse similarly shaped letters such as b and d, and p and q. Although a correct diagnosis can be made only by an expert, the following may help you to recognize dyslexia in your child:
• Poor co-ordination.
• Difficulty in remembering lists of words, numbers or letters.
• Difficulty in remembering the order of everyday things, such as days of the week.
• Problems telling left from right.
• Jumbled phrases, such as "tebby dare" instead of "teddy bear".
• Difficulty learning nursery rhymes.
• At school age, poor spelling.
A special test to diagnose dyslexia exists for preschool children. The test involves repeating nonsense words, matching a series of pictures, identifying rhyming words and testing balance and reaction.

EFFECTS OF DYSLEXIA

The problems listed above may occur in children who don't have dyslexia. The difference is that dyslexic children will suffer more severe symptoms and won't grow out of them.

Recent research suggests that as well as having problems with literacy, dyslexic children also have problems with distinguishing different sounds, and with memory and balance. For example, dyslexic children will find it much more difficult to balance on one leg than children who don't have dyslexia.

A dyslexic child's strengths are likely to be sensitivity, intuition and impulsiveness. Skills associated with the left side of the brain, such as dealing with written symbols, responding to instructions and putting things in order, are weak in the dyslexic child. Some dyslexic children may be very creative and have an aptitude for drawing and painting.

SPECIAL NEEDS

One of the main problems that dyslexic children face is incorrect diagnosis. It is common for children to attempt to learn to read and write, fail to do so and then be labelled "slow" or even disabled. This is very demoralizing for the child and is bound to affect his school performance overall. Parents and teachers often confuse dyslexia with a low IQ, but in fact most children with dyslexia have an average or above-average IQ.

If dyslexia is recognized early, remedial education is very effective. If a child is diagnosed as dyslexic at the age of four or five, when he goes to school, he will probably need only about half-an-hour's extra tuition a day for a period of six months to bring his reading and writing up to normal standards. If dyslexia is not diagnosed until he's seven or eight, he will have a lot of catching up to do.

HOW YOU CAN HELP

You can do three things to help your dyslexic child at home. First – and this is sometimes overlooked – acknowledge that your child actually has a problem. If you are told that your child will catch up or will learn to read eventually, don't listen: dyslexia is a specific learning disorder that will respond only to the appropriate remedial treatment. Second, be supportive and positive, especially if your child is having problems at school. Third, play lots of learning games with your child. *Emotional support* If your child is at school and is lagging behind other children, his self-confidence may be low and it is very important that you make

him feel successful at home. Don't show any impatience. Encourage him to do the things that he is good at and help him do things for himself.

Give him self-help aids, such as left and right stickers on his tricycle, and, if he finds a particular task difficult tell him to take it slowly. The British Dyslexia Association (see Useful addresses, p. 93) gives advice on coping strategies and remedial education for dyslexic children.

Home learning games Playing games with letters, words and sounds can be very useful. The following are all ways in which you can have fun with your child and enhance his learning:

• Say nursery rhymes aloud together or make up rhyming poems or limericks. This will familiarize your child with the concept of rhyming words.
• Teach your child rhymes or songs that involve sequences of things, for example, days of the week.
• Play "Simon Says". This will help your child to follow instructions.
• Play "Hunt the Thimble". This will encourage your child to ask questions involving concepts such as under, on, above and inside.
• Introduce the concept of left and right.
• Ask your child to lay the table for meals.
• Play clapping games. Give one clap for each syllable of a word and get your child to repeat it. Clap a rhythm to his name.
• Give your child groups of words and ask him to pick out the odd word.
• Get your child to think of as many words as he can that begin with a particular letter.
• Play "I Spy". If your child has difficulty with letter names, make the sound of the letter instead.
• Encourage your child to trace words and letters, or to make letters out of plasticine.

ASTHMA

About one in seven children in the UK has asthma. Hospital admissions for asthma have been increasing steeply in young children and admission rates have doubled since the mid-1970s.

A child who has asthma will suffer recurrent attacks of breathlessness with wheezing when he tries to exhale. These attacks are caused by narrowing of the small airways in the lungs. They vary greatly in severity but even a mild attack can be frightening in a young child. Over 50 percent of children affected by asthma grow out of the condition by adulthood.

HOW YOU CAN HELP

Although there is no known cure for asthma, modern asthma management can effectively allow your child to lead a full life. Regular contact with your doctor and close monitoring of your child are vital.

Your doctor will develop an asthma management plan with you, and explain when to use the *preventer* and *reliever*, and what to do if your child's symptoms get worse. This should be written down for you to keep at home. A vital part of any plan is a review meeting with a doctor or nurse trained in asthma management every few months. Consult your doctor if you notice any of the following:
• Wheezing and coughing in the early morning.
• Increased symptoms after exercise or exertion.
• Waking at night with a cough or a wheeze.
• Increased use of the reliever.
An emergency plan Any asthma attack can be life-threatening, so be sure to have an emergency plan of action agreed with your doctor for very severe attacks.

• At the start of the attack give your child his usual reliever. Wait about ten minutes and, if there is no improvement, send for an ambulance.
• Repeat the treatment until the breathing symptoms improve or until help arrives.
• Give your child steroid tablets if they've been prescribed by your doctor.
• Keep your child in an upright position.
• Call your doctor or an ambulance or take your child to the nearest hospital.

CYSTIC FIBROSIS

An inherited condition, cystic fibrosis (CF) produces thick and sticky mucus in the lungs and the pancreas. CF is the most common inherited disease of its kind in the UK and affects approximately one in every 2,500 children (boys and girls in equal numbers), although to differing degrees. The gene responsible for CF has now been discovered and there is a chance that there will be a cure by the time your child reaches adulthood.

WHEN TO SEE THE DOCTOR

Your CF child is very vulnerable to chest infections, so it's important to seek medical help promptly, either from your doctor or your child's regular hospital clinic, if you think something is wrong. The following symptoms may indicate that a doctor's visit is needed:
• Decreased or poor appetite.
• Weight loss.
• Tummy aches.
• Frequent or loose stools.
• Increased or frequent cough.
• Vomiting.
• Increased sputum or change in its colour.
• Breathlessness.
• Unwillingness to exercise.
• Fever.
• Common cold symptoms.

DIABETES MELLITUS

A chronic disease, diabetes mellitus in children is due to a lack of insulin, which is produced in the pancreas. Insufficient insulin results in an increase in blood glucose concentration (hyperglycaemia), causing excessive urination and constant thirst and hunger. An accumulation in the body of chemicals called ketones occurs when there is a severe lack of insulin. A high sugar level is not in itself dangerous, but high ketone levels are.

The onset of diabetes can be swift and may take some time to stabilize. Most diabetic children need insulin injections and a strictly controlled diet, so discuss all aspects with your doctor.

HOW YOU CAN HELP

You will need to exercise skill to help your child accept his condition with the least fuss. You should supervise invisibly, while giving your child responsibility to learn self-care and control.

Children with diabetes tend to worry more than children without the disease, and this is only to be expected; they have to assume important responsibilities and they know, or will come to know, that diabetes can do some very unpleasant things. Diabetes makes children feel tired and confused, and can make them lose consciousness. A child who is diabetic has to plan ahead when leaving home, and remember to take along some sweets or sugar and insulin and syringes if the trip is a long one. Your child is threatened both physically and psychologically by diabetes, so you need to be sympathetic without becoming over-protective. As your child grows older, however, he will gain mastery over the situation, learn self-care and understand what needs to be done.

CEREBRAL PALSY

Cerebral palsy is caused by an injury to the brain, usually before, around or soon after the time of birth. Occasionally, the brain is formed abnormally for no obvious reason, or the disorder is inherited even if both parents are healthy.

If a child has cerebral palsy it means that part of the child's brain either is not working properly or has not developed normally. The affected area is usually one of the parts of the brain that controls the muscles and certain body movements; the disease interferes with the messages that normally pass from the brain to the body. In some children cerebral palsy is hardly noticeable at all; others are more severely affected. No two children will be affected in quite the same way.

HOW YOU CAN HELP

• Your child may get stiffer and have more muscle spasm when he's lying on his back, so lay him on his side or tummy instead, supporting him with a cushion if necessary. It's also a good idea to change his position every 20 minutes or so.

• Help your child to learn to use his hands right from the start by letting him feel things with different textures, and encouraging him to hold toys and other objects. Toys securely strung over his chair can be useful.

• Enable your child to learn shapes by showing him different simply shaped objects, and encouraging him to handle them and play with them.

• A cerebral palsy child of three or four years may want to help with everyday tasks around the house like any child of the same age. Explain to your child what you're doing, let him watch you and if possible let him join in.

EPILEPSY

The most common disease of the brain in the UK, epilepsy affects 1 in 200 births and tends to run in families. The normal electrical impulses in the brain are disturbed, causing periodic seizures which can be very minor or severe. There are several forms of epileptic seizure. Grand mal involves convulsions with loss of consciousness. In petit mal, there are no convulsions, only a second or two of unconsciousness, rather like day-dreaming.

WHAT TO DO DURING A SEIZURE

• Remove any furniture, so that your child's jerking limbs don't hit solid objects.
• Loosen the clothing around your child's neck or chest.
• Don't try to hold your child's teeth apart if they are clenched, and don't put anything into his mouth.
• As soon as your child stops moving violently, put him in the recovery position (see p. 90).
• During a petit mal seizure, guide your child to safety and stay with him until it has passed.
• Make a note of what happens during a seizure so that you can tell your doctor.

HOW YOU CAN HELP

You should never stop your child's medication without first seeking medical advice. Treat your child as normally as possible all the time. He should always wear a bracelet or medallion engraved with information about his epilepsy.

SICKLE CELL DISEASE

This inherited disease is caused by an abnormality of haemoglobin, the oxygen-carrying substance in red blood cells. It is most common in people of African or West Indian descent, but may also occur in people from the Indian subcontinent, the Middle East and the eastern Mediterranean. A child with sickle cell disease (SCD) will be prone to bouts of violent and unpredictable pain and may be at risk from other disorders, but most of the time he will be quite well.

HOW YOU CAN HELP

Although knowledge about the disease is incomplete, you must be as well informed as possible, so that you can help your child avoid pain crises. Counselling will give you a safe, confidential way to explore your feelings, and provide encouragement and support (see Useful Addresses, p. 93).

When your child starts school, you should inform all of his teachers about his condition, making them aware of the problems it can impose on his education, for example, your child may miss out on classes because of hospital admissions or a crisis. Reassure your child and encourage him to express his feelings and anxieties.

Your child's feelings must be given great consideration. Many children with SCD can experience difficulties with their classmates. Your child's teachers should educate the other children about SCD so that your child does not suffer from feelings of alienation or isolation – as he might if, for example, they thought they could catch the disease from him.

Many SCD children express a fear of dying or being deformed. Others feel they're the only ones who are suffering from this condition and that nobody understands them. Some are afraid of expressing when they are in pain in case nobody believes them. You can help enormously by making sure that your child feels assured of your understanding, sympathy and care whenever he needs it.

FIRST AID

As a parent, you will inevitably have to cope with minor accidents as your child grows up. Most of the time these will be minor cuts and bruises, but you should be equipped to cope with major accidents or emergencies, should they occur. All parents should know the basic first aid techniques to deal with accidents quickly, effectively and calmly. To give first aid effectively you need to understand and practise the techniques detailed on the following pages, and you should also keep a first aid kit in your home. This should be accessible in an emergency but stored out of reach of your child.

EMERGENCY FIRST AID

A severe accident with the loss of much blood or other body fluids may precipitate shock, which is always serious. Other emergencies include choking (see p. 92), a very severe respiratory tract infection that blocks the airways, drowning and unconsciousness. Prompt action on your part can be lifesaving.

HOME FIRST AID KIT

You can buy a ready-made home first aid kit from any pharmacy, but putting your own together is easy and inexpensive. Store the items in an airtight, waterproof container.

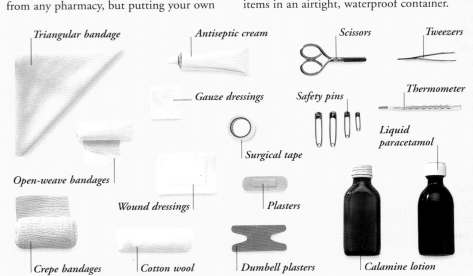

Triangular bandage

Antiseptic cream

Scissors

Tweezers

Gauze dressings

Safety pins

Thermometer

Liquid paracetamol

Surgical tape

Open-weave bandages

Wound dressings

Plasters

Crepe bandages

Cotton wool

Dumbell plasters

Calamine lotion

PRIORITIES

When your child has an accident you must get your priorities right. Tell any adult present to call an ambulance while you go through the following checklist. Detailed instructions are shown for resuscitation (see pp. 90–92) and choking (see p. 92). If there isn't anyone to help, you should go through the checklist before calling an ambulance (see below).

Is your child in danger? If appropriate, remove your child from the danger, or the danger from your child. Do not put yourself at risk, and do not move your child if you suspect a fracture.

Is he conscious? Shake your child gently by his shoulders and keep calling his name.

Is his airway blocked? Open your child's airway by supporting the chin and tilting the head back. Then clear any obstruction (see p. 92).

Is he breathing? Lean close to your child's mouth to listen for breathing and feel his breath against your cheek. Look at his chest to see if it is rising and falling. If there are no signs of breathing after five seconds, give five breaths of ventilation (see p. 91).

Does he have a pulse? Check for a pulse in the arm or neck (see p. 91), or place your hand on your child's chest and count the beats. A normal pulse rate is about 120 beats per minute for a baby and 100–120 beats per minute for a one-year-old. If no pulse is present, or if the pulse is less than 60 beats per minute in a baby, give alternate chest compressions (see p. 92) and ventilation (see p. 91) for one minute, call an ambulance, taking your child with you to the telephone if you can, then continue resuscitation.

Call an ambulance If your child is having breathing difficulties or is unconscious, then call an ambulance, or get another adult to do so. Try not to leave your child unattended and be prepared to carry out resuscitation on him. When calling an ambulance, state your name clearly and give your exact location: the road name and house number or name, including any junctions or landmarks, and your telephone number. Describe the condition of your child and give his age, and tell the operator if you are a qualified First Aider. You should also give details of any hazards, such as a gas leak, or relevant local weather conditions, for example fog or icy roads.

FIRST AID TRAINING

You must learn the first aid procedures on these pages by heart in order to make use of them. If you have to waste time referring to this book to refresh your memory, your delay could be the difference between life and death.

This book cannot make you a "First Aider". To learn first aid properly you should complete a course of instruction and pass a professionally supervised examination. The Standard First Aid Certificate is awarded by the St. John Ambulance, St. Andrew's Ambulance Association and the British Red Cross (see Useful Addresses, p. 93). It is valid for only three years, after which you should update your skills with further training.

THE ABC OF RESUSCITATION

If your child stops breathing or loses consciousness, you must carry out the following checks in the order given:

A is for Airway *Open the airway, look in the mouth and check for obstructions. Clear the airway if you can by tilting your child's head back.*

B is for Breathing *If your child shows no signs of breathing you will have to breathe for him with ventilations (see opposite).*

C is for Circulation *Check that your child has a pulse. If there is none or if it is very weak, you will have to give chest compressions (see p. 92) and ventilation (see opposite).*

RESUSCITATION

The body's vital organs need a continuous supply of oxygen. If any part of the process by which oxygen is carried to body cells and tissues goes wrong, unconsciousness may result. Air must be inhaled to supply oxygen to the blood, and the oxygenated blood must be pumped around the body by the heart. If the brain is deprived of oxygen for more than three minutes, it will begin to fail. If the heart fails, death will occur unless emergency action is taken. Resuscitation is necessary if, for whatever reason, your child has stopped breathing or if his pulse has stopped (see opposite).

If your child has lost consciousness and isn't breathing, he's at risk of brain damage and heart failure. You need to assess his condition quickly in order to know what first aid treatment to give. If he's unconscious but still breathing and has a pulse, then you should call for help and place him in the recovery position. If he's unconscious and not breathing but has a pulse, you will need to give artificial ventilation (see opposite). If he's not breathing and has no pulse, you must give ventilation and chest compressions (see pp. 91 and 92).

THE RECOVERY POSITION

An unconscious child who is still breathing and has a regular pulse should be placed in this position to keep the airway open and to allow liquids to drain from the mouth. You should not place your child in the recovery position if you suspect a fracture.

The uppermost leg should be bent at a right angle so that the hip and knee act as a "prop"

Place the arm at right angles to the body with the elbow bent

1 If your child is lying on his back or side, kneel to one side of him. Straighten his legs and gently place the arm nearest you at right angles to his body with the elbow bent.

2 Ensure that the head is tilted back throughout the procedure so that the airway remains open. Bring the other arm across the chest and place the back of the hand so that it lies against the cheek.

3 Still pressing your child's hand to his cheek, grasp the far thigh and pull the knee up. Keep the foot flat on the ground and place it next to the nearer knee.

4 Roll your child over into a resting position with his knee bent and his head resting on his hand.

ASSESSING A TODDLER

1 Check for consciousness
See if your child is conscious by shaking him gently and pinching him. Keep calling his name. If he doesn't respond, call for help straight away.

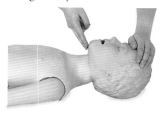

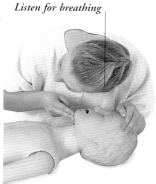

Listen for breathing

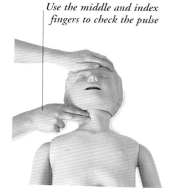

Use the middle and index fingers to check the pulse

2 Clear the airway
Look in the mouth to see if it is obstructed. If it is, clear it with your fingers, but take care not to push it further in. Open the airway by putting two fingers under your child's chin and lifting the jaw. Tilt the head back by placing your other hand on his forehead.

3 Check breathing
Look, listen and feel for signs of breathing. Look along the chest and abdomen for movements; listen for sounds of breathing; and feel for your child's breath on your cheek. If he is not breathing, give five breaths of artificial ventilation, then check his pulse.

4 Check the pulse
See if your child's heart is still beating by placing your fingers just in front of the large muscle at the side of the neck under the angle of the jaw. If there's no pulse, give him one minute of chest compressions and ventilation (see p. 92), call an ambulance, then continue.

ARTIFICIAL VENTILATION FOR TODDLERS

If your child has stopped breathing

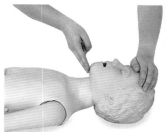

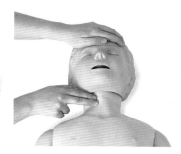

1 Open the airway
Lay your child down on his back on a firm surface. Check there is nothing obstructing the mouth or throat – if there is, carefully remove it, but don't stick your finger down your child's throat. Place two fingers under his chin and tilt his head back.

2 Give ventilation
Using your finger and thumb, pinch your child's nostrils closed. Inhale, put your mouth over his mouth, making a complete seal, and breathe out until his chest rises. Remove your mouth and watch the chest fall. Give one breath every three seconds.

3 Check the pulse
After one minute of ventilation, check the pulse in your child's neck (see above). If there is no pulse, give chest compressions (see p. 92) and ventilation for one minute, then call an ambulance. If there is, continue ventilation; check the pulse every minute.

CHEST COMPRESSION FOR TODDLERS
If there is no pulse, give chest compressions with ventilation

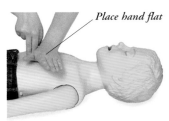
Place hand flat

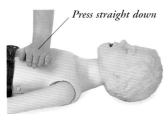
Press straight down

1 Positioning the hand
Place your child on his back on a firm surface. Put the middle finger of one hand on the tip of the breastbone (the bone where the ribs meet in the middle), and the index finger above it. Put the heel of your other hand so that it rests just above the index finger.

2 Give chest compressions
Take your fingers away from the breastbone and, using the heel of the other hand, press down sharply to a depth of about 3 centimetres (1¼ inches). Give five compressions in three seconds (time them with the second hand of a clock or watch).

3 Give artificial ventilation
After five compressions give one breath of ventilation (see p. 91). Don't stop to take your child's pulse unless he shows signs of reviving. Alternate five compressions in three seconds with one breath of ventilation. After one minute, call an ambulance, then continue.

CHOKING

If your child's airway becomes partially or completely blocked, he will choke and, if he's unable to get enough oxygen into his lungs, may lose consciousness. To restore normal breathing, the blockage must be removed. You need to act promptly. Follow the steps outlined below to remove the obstruction. If, after following these steps, you are unable to clear the obstruction, you should call an ambulance immediately.

1 Get him to cough
Encourage your child to cough as this will help to dislodge the obstruction.

2 Back slaps
If the obstruction is still there or he seems to be weakening, bend him forwards, stand behind him and to the side and slap him sharply five times between the shoulder blades with the flat of your hand. Check his mouth to see if the blockage is visible, but don't stick your finger down his throat. If the back slaps fail, give him chest thrusts (see step 3).

Position a clenched fist, with the thumb on the breastbone, for a chest thrust

Place a fist thumb inwards, below the rib cage for an abdominal thrust

3 Chest thrusts
Stand or kneel behind your child. Make a fist and place this over the centre of his chest, cover this with your other hand and give five sharp inward thrusts. Check the mouth.

4 Abdominal thrusts
If the blockage is still there, make a fist, place this below the rib cage and make five upward thrusts. Check the mouth. If the blockage is still there, call an ambulance. Repeat the above sequence until help arrives. If he loses consciousness be ready to resuscitate (see pp. 90–91).

USEFUL ADDRESSES

ADVICE AND SUPPORT

MAMA (Meet-a-Mum Association)
Waterside Centre
25 Avenue Road
London SE25 4DX
Tel: 020 8768 0123
For isolated or depressed mothers

PARENTS' GROUPS

Multiple Births Foundation
Hammersmith House – Level 4
Queen Charlotte and Chelsea
Hospital
Du Cane Road
London W12 0HS
Tel: 020 8383 3519

National Council for One-Parent Families
255 Kentish Town Road
London NW5 2LX
Tel: 020 7267 1361

Parentline Plus
520 Highgate Studios
53–79 Highgate Road
Kentish Town
London NW5 1TL
Tel: 0808 800 2222
Helpline for all ages

TAMBA (Twins and Multiple Birth Association)
Harnott House
309 Chester Road
Little Sutton
Ellesmere Port,
Chester CH66 1QQ
Tel: 0870 121 4000

CARE AND EDUCATION

National Childminding Association
8 Masons Hill
Bromley
Kent BR2 9EY
Tel: 020 8464 6164

Preschool Learning Alliance
61–63 King's Cross Road
London WC1X 9LL
Tel: 020 7833 0991

FIRST AID AND SAFETY

British Red Cross
9 Grosvenor Crescent
London SW1X 7EJ
Tel: 020 7235 5454

Child Accident Prevention Trust
18–20 Farringdon Lane
London EC1R 3HA
Tel: 020 7608 3828

Royal Society for the Prevention of Accidents (RoSPA)
Edgbaston Park
353 Bristol Road
Birmingham B5 7ST
Tel: 0121 748 2000

St. Andrew's Ambulance Association
St. Andrew's House
48 Milton Street
Cowcaddans
Glasgow G4 0HR
Tel: 0141 332 4031

St. John Ambulance
1 Grosvenor Crescent
London SW1X 7EF
Tel: 0870 2355231

CHILDREN WITH SPECIAL NEEDS

British Stammering Association
15 Old Ford Road
Bethnal Green
London E2 9PJ
Helpline: 020 8983 1003

British Dyslexia Association
98 London Road
Reading
Berks RG1 5AU
Tel: 0118 9668271

British Epilepsy Association
New Anstey House
Gate Way Drive
Yeadon, Leeds LS19 7XY
Tel: 01132 108800
Support from local groups

Contact-a-Family
209–211 City Road
London EC1V 1JN
Tel: 020 7608 8700
Supports parents of children with special needs

Cystic Fibrosis Trust
Alexandra House
11 London Road
Bromley
Kent BR1 1BY
Tel: 020 8464 7211

Diabetes UK (formerly the British Diabetic Association)
10 Queen Anne Street
London W1G 9LH
Tel: 020 7323 1531

Down's Syndrome Association
155 Mitcham Road
London SW17 9PG
Tel: 020 8682 4001

MENCAP (The Royal Society for Mentally Handicapped Children and Adults)
Mencap National Centre
123 Golden Lane
London EC1Y 0RT
Tel: 020 7454 0454
For people with learning disabilities

The National Asthma Campaign
Providence House
Providence Place
London N1 0NT
Tel: 0845 7010203

The National Eczema Society
Hill House
Highgate Hill
London N19 5NA
Tel: 0870 241 3604

Scope
6 Market Road
London N7 9PW
Helpline: 0808 800 3333
Support, assessment and education for people with cerebral palsy

The Sickle Cell Society
54 Station Road
Harlesden
London NW10 4UA
Tel: 020 8961 7795
Send sae for information leaflets

INDEX

A

access, divorced parents, 68
accidents, 88–92
adenoids, 75
adoption, 49
affection, 27
allergies, 11, 12
ambulances, 89
appetite, loss of, 70
asthma, 85

B

babies, 24–25, 53
balance, 37, 38
bathing, 14, 16–17
beds, 28–29, 72
bedtimes, 26, 29
bedwetting, 21, 22
bladder control, 20–23
bowel control, 20–23
boys:
    behaviour, 50
    cleanliness, 17
    development, 33
    dressing, 19
    language development,
        47, 48
    mental development, 42
    weight, 9
brain:
    cerebral palsy, 86
    development, 33, 41–42
    dyslexia, 83-4
    epilepsy, 87
    female, 41
    male, 42
breastfeeding, 62
breathing, emergencies,
    70, 89–92

C

car journeys, 60–61
cerebral palsy, 86
chairs, portable, 10
chest compression, 92
chickenpox, 77
child care, 57, 62, 63
childminders, 63
choking, 92
"clingy" children, 26–27
clothes, 18–19, 39–40
colds, 76
colours, 44
concepts, forming, 44
constipation, 22–23
convulsions, 73, 87
cots, 28
coughs, 76–77
crafts, 40
crawling, 32
creativity, 42
crèches, 63
crying, 24–25
cuddles, 26–27
cystic fibrosis, 85

D

dark, fear of, 30
day nurseries, 63
dental care, 15
diabetes mellitus, 86
diarrhoea, 70
diphtheria, 79, 80
diseases, 77–80
divorce, 66–68
doctor, when to call, 70–71
drawing, 40, 43
dressing, 18–19, 39–40
dribbling, 82

drinks, sick children, 72, 73
dyslexia, 83–84
    home learning games, 84

E

ear infections, 74
eczema, 75–76
education, preschool, 63–65
emergencies, 71, 88–92
    choking, 92
    recovery position, 90
epilepsy, 87
eyesight, 32

F

faddy eaters, 10
fathers, 53, 57
fears, 24, 30
febrile convulsions, 73
fevers, 70, 71, 73
first aid, 88–92
food, 8–13
food intolerance, 11–12
food preferences, 10
friends, 50–53

G

German measles (rubella),
    78, 80
girls:
    behaviour, 49
    cleanliness, 16
    development, 32
    dressing, 18
    language development,
        46, 48
    mental development, 41
    weight, 8

ACKNOWLEDGMENTS

Dorling Kindersley would like to thank the following individuals and organizations for their contribution to this book:

PHOTOGRAPHY
All photographs by Jules Selmes, except Susanna Price for the title page

ILLUSTRATION
Aziz Khan

MEDICAL CONSULTANTS
Dr. Margaret Lawson, Dr. Frances Williams

EQUIPMENT
Boots the Chemist, Children's World, Debenham's, Freeman's Mail Order

ADDITIONAL EDITORIAL AND DESIGN ASSISTANCE
Nicky Adamson, Claire Cross, David Summers, Ruth Tomkins

DTP ASSISTANCE
Rajen Shah

INDEX
Hilary Bird

TEXT FILM
The Brightside Partnership, London